International Challenges to American Colleges and Universities

Looking Ahead

Edited by
Katharine H. Hanson
and Joel W. Meyerson

AMERICAN COUNCIL
ON EDUCATION
Series on Higher Education
ORYX PRESS
1995

The rare Arabian Oryx is believed to have inspired the myth of the unicorn. This desert
antelope became virtually extinct in the early 1960s. At that time several groups of
international conservationists arranged to have 9 animals sent to the Phoenix Zoo
to be the nucleus of a captive breeding herd. Today the Oryx population
is over 800 and nearly 400 have been returned to reserves
in the Middle East.

© 1995 by American Council on Education and The Oryx Press
Published by the Oryx Press
4041 North Central at Indian School Road
Phoenix, Arizona 85012-3397

Published simultaneously in Canada
Printed and Bound in the United States of America

❂ The paper used in this publication meets the minimum requirements of
American National Standard for Information Science—Permanence of Paper
for Printed Library Materials, ANSI Z39.48, 1984.

Library of Congress Cataloging-in-Publication Data

International challenges to American colleges and universities : looking ahead / edited
by Katharine H. Hanson and Joel W. Meyerson.
   p.   cm. — (American Council on Education/Oryx series on higher education)
Papers from a symposium held in the fall of 1992.
Includes bibliographical references and index.
ISBN 0-89774-868-9
   1. International education—United States—Congresses.   2. Education, Higher—
United States—Aims and objectives—Congresses.   I. Hanson, Katharine.   II.
Meyerson, Joel W., 1951– .   III. Series.
LC1090.I5516   1994
370.11'5'0973—dc20   94-30378
                                                                                              CIP

Contents

❖ ❖ ❖ ❖ ❖ ❖ ❖ ❖

iii

Preface

❀ ❀ ❀ ❀ ❀ ❀ ❀ ❀ ❀

Our entire society is undergoing fundamental change that is likely to surpass in scope and velocity the change wrought by the dawn of the Industrial Age over a century ago. This change is being driven, in large measure, by the accelerating globalization of our economic, intellectual, and cultural institutions. Surprisingly, American higher education, itself a cauldron of social and scientific discovery, has largely been immune to this trend. This too is bound to change.

The symposium on "International Challenges for American Higher Education" was organized to explore ideas and encourage more thinking about global education. It brought together a small group of leading university and college presidents, trustees, international scholars, foundation heads, and government policymakers to discuss the opportunities—*and threats*—inherent in this new environment. On one issue, consensus quickly emerged: at the very moment when more resources are needed to fund international research programs, traditional sources of support—the federal government and national foundations—are retreating.

The chapters in this book reflect the papers presented at the symposium as well as the spirited discussion that followed. Together, these papers address many of the key issues in international higher education. Much research remains to be done, however. Areas of future inquiry include identifying the national, political, and legal impediments to international collaboration; assessing the impact of expansion of higher education in other nations on student flows to and from the U.S.; determining how corporate funding of research will change in response to new funding opportunities abroad; and estimating the cost of international collaboration and comparing its benefits with domestic activities.

The scholarship and insights in this volume represent an important step forward in understanding how globalization is transforming American higher education.

JWM and KHH

Contributors

❖ ❖ ❖ ❖ ❖ ❖ ❖ ❖

Michael Aiken is the chancellor at the University of Illinois, Urbana-Champaign. He was formerly provost and professor of sociology at the University of Pennsylvania. During his two years as dean of the School of Arts and Sciences at Penn, he led the faculty in developing an SAS five-year plan and in overhauling undergraduate distributional requirements. In 1987, Dr. Aiken became Penn's 25th Provost and led the faculty in setting priorities for the University's next five-year plan.

Before going to Penn, Dr. Aiken taught for 11 years at the University of Wisconsin, where he rose through the ranks from assistant professor in 1963 to professor in 1970. He served as associate dean of the College of Arts and Letters there from 1980 to 82. During those years, he also held visiting professorships at Columbia University, Washington (St. Louis), and on four separate occasions at University of Louvain in Belgium.

In addition to serving on the boards of seven journals, Chancellor Aiken has published several books and more than 40 articles on a wide range of sociological topics, including organizational behavior, community structure, and political sociology.

Lewis Branscomb is Albert Pratt Public Service Professor at the John F. Kennedy School of Government of Harvard University and directs the school's Science Technology and Public Policy Program in the Center for Science and International Affairs.

Previously, Dr. Branscomb was vice president and chief scientist of International Business Machines Corporation. He was also a member of the Corporate Management Board and a director of the IBM World Trade Europe/

Africa Corporation. In addition, Dr. Branscomb has served on numerous boards and is a member of several professional associations. His presidential appointments include the National Science Board, President Johnson's Science Advisory Committee, the President's Commission for the Medal of Science, and President Reagan's National Productivity Advisory Committee.

He has been past president of the American Physical Society and of Sigma Xi, the Scientific Research Society. He has served on the U.S. Department of State's Advisory Committee on Science and Foreign Affairs and is a former member of the Board of Directors of the American Association for the Advancement of Science. A former chairman of the Committee on Scholarly Communications with the People's Republic of China, he is a member of the National Research Council's Committee on Japan Affairs.

Colin Campbell is president of the Rockefeller Brothers Fund, a grantmaking program that emphasizes the concept of global interdependence. The Fund engages in considerable amount of international grantmaking, concentrated in the two areas of sustainable resource use and world security. Previously, Mr. Campbell served as president of Wesleyan University for 18 years. Before going to Wesleyan, he was a vice president of the Planning and Government Affairs Division of the American Stock Exchange. In addition to his professional positions, Mr. Campbell has also been a member of several educational commissions and associations, including the Commission on the University of the Twenty-first Century in Virginia and the Governor's Commission on Equity and Excellence in Education in Connecticut. He is also a former chairman of the Consortium on Financing Higher Education and served as president of the New England Association of Schools and Colleges.

Gerhard Friedrich is president of his own consulting firm and has worked with Rosabeth Kanter at Goodmeasure, Inc., a Cambridge management consulting firm. He is a former executive consultant for Digital Equipment Corporation where he focused primarily on higher education. He also served as Digital's executive partner to Harvard University and the Dun and Bradstreet Corporation. Other positions he held at Digital included director of Corporate Executive Marketing and director of Technology Transfer, part of Digital's Artificial Technology Center.

His teaching positions have included an appointment as a visiting behavior scientist at MIT's Sloan School of Business as part of the "Management in the 1990s" Research Program. Prior to Digital, he held management positions at Corning Glass Works, the Bell System, Addressograph/Multigraph, and Sherwin-Williams. He has served as lecturer to a broad range of professional associations, at a number of leading universities, and as a member of the graduate faculty at the University of New Haven.

Fred M. Hayward is the senior associate for International Initiatives at the American Council on Education. Prior to joining ACE, he served as a consultant for the government of Sierra Leone, advising them on the transition from a one-party state to a multi-party system. He also worked with the International Foundation for Electoral Systems, and the AID Center for University Cooperation in Development.

Mr. Hayward spent a good part of his career at the University of Wisconsin, beginning as an instructor in 1967 and serving as a full professor from 1978 until 1991. He served in several administrative capacities at the University of Wisconsin, including acting dean for International Studies and Programs, and chair for both the departments of Political Science and the African Studies Program.

He has lectured and written numerous articles on African politics, particularly relating to the Sierra Leone, and is a member of the American Political Science Association, the African Studies Association and the Midwest Political Science Association Joint Center for Political and Economic Studies.

Richard D. Lambert is the founder and former director (retired in 1993) of the National Foreign Language Center in Washington, D.C. He spent many years of distinguished academic service at the University of Pennsylvania, serving at various times as dean of Instruction and Academic Planning, dean of the College of General Studies, and chair of the Department of South Asia Regional Studies. Most recently, he was a professor of comparative sociology at the Lauder Institute of International Management.

His professional service has included leadership roles in such academic and professional organizations as the Association for Asian Studies, the American Academy of Political and Social Science, the Social Science Research Council, the Center for Applied Linguistics, and the American Institute of Indian Studies. Also, he has served in advisory roles to the U.S. Department of Education, the Department of Defense, and the United Nations Economic, Social, and Cultural Commission. He is currently a member of the New York State Curriculum and Assessment Committee for Language other than English and the advisory board of the AT&T Language Line.

Stephen R. Lewis, Jr., is president and professor of economics at Carleton College. He previously served Williams College as the Herbert H. Lehman Professor of Economics and in a number of administrative leadership positions, including chairman of the economics department and provost of the College.

Dr. Lewis has worked and traveled extensively as an economic advisor and consultant for many countries and organizations, including the Ministry of Finance and Development Planning of Botswana since 1975, the Ministry of Finance and Economic Planning of Kenya, the Pakistan Institute of Development Economics, the OECD Development Center, the World Bank, USAID, the Ford Foundation, the government of the Philippines, and the East African Community. He is a member of the Council on Foreign Relations, a trustee for the Carnegie Endowment for International Peace, and a former editor for the *Journal of Economic Literature.*

Richard Lyman is president emeritus and emeritus J.E. Wallace Sterling Professor of Humanities in the Department of History at Stanford University. He previously held positions as professor of history, associate dean of the School of Humanities and Sciences, and vice president and provost at Stanford. After leaving Stanford, he served as president of the Rockefeller Foundation, and then as director of the Institute for International Studies at Stanford University until his retirement in 1991.

Dr. Lyman has served as director of the Council on Foundations and chaired the board of Independent Sector; he is a past chairman of the Association of American Universities. He currently serves as a director of the National Committee on United States-China Relations, the International Business Machines Corporation, and the World Affairs Council of Northern California. He is also a member of the American Historical Association and the Council on Foreign Relations.

Steven Muller is chairman of the 21st Century Foundation and president emeritus of the Johns Hopkins University. He is Distinguished Professorial Lecturer at the Paul H. Nitze School of Advanced International Studies of the Johns Hopkins University in Washington, D.C.

Dr. Muller is director and trustee of a number of corporations and educational and cultural institutions. He is vice chairman of the board of trustees of the American Institute for Contemporary German Studies, a director of the Atlantic Council, and a Fellow of the American Academy of Arts and Sciences. He is also a member of the American Association of Rhodes Scholars, the Council on Foreign Relations, and the International Institute for Strategic Studies.

In past years, Dr. Muller served as a member and chairman of the Association of American Universities; founding chairman of the National Association of Independent Colleges and Universities; a director of the Council on Financial Aid to Education; and a member of two presidential commissions. He served as chairman of the task force on NASA-University Relations and was a member of the board of editors of *Daedalus,* a trustee of the German Marshal Fund, a director of the Whitney Museum of American Art, a director of the Baltimore Museum of Art, a trustee of the Consortium for the Advancement of Private Higher Education, and he served twice as a director of the Greater Baltimore Committee.

Charles Vest is president of MIT. He previously served as provost and vice president for Academic Affairs at the University of Michigan.

Dr. Vest is a professor of mechanical engineering and an authority on holographic interferometry, which is the application of optical holography to visualize or precisely measure thermal and mechanical phenomena.

Dr. Vest also serves as a trustee or corporation member of the Boston Museum of Science, Environmental Research Institute of Michigan, New England Aquarium, Wellesley College, WGBH Educational Foundation (*ex officio*), and Woods Hole Oceanographic Institution. He is a director of DuPont. He is a member of the Executive Committee of the Council on Competitiveness, the Governor's Task Force on Economic Growth and Technology of the Commonwealth of Massachusetts, the National Research Council Board on Engineering Education, and the Ronald E. McNair Foundation Advisory Board.

Gareth Williams is a professor of educational administration and chairman of the Department of Policy Studies at the Institute of Education at the University of London. He also heads the Center for Higher Education Studies. His previous posts have included professor of educational planning and director for the Institute for Research and Development in Post-Compulsory Education at Lancaster University; joint director, Higher Education Research Unit, London School of Economics; and principal administrator and directorate for scientific affairs for the Organization for Economic Cooperation and Development.

Dr. Williams is a frequent consultant for the OECD, UNESCO, the World Bank, the International Labour Office, and other national and international organizations. Dr. Williams is also the planning editor for the *International Journal of Higher Education and Education Planning* and coeditor of *Higher Education Quarterly.* He is widely published on topics relating to the funding and financing of higher education.

Introduction

❧ ❧ ❧ ❧ ❧ ❧ ❧ ❧ ❧

Profound changes in national economies and politics are driving change in educational systems around the world. Coupled with increased regional and intercontinental educational compacts, these changes present both new opportunities and new risks for academic institutions in the United States. A symposium on "International Challenges for American Higher Education" was organized in the fall of 1992 by MIT, the Consortium on Financing Higher Education (COFHE), and Coopers & Lybrand. The purpose of the symposium was to identify the forces that will shape the "global university" of the future and to begin charting effective strategies to meet the challenges of the dynamic international environment. This book contains the papers and findings presented at that symposium.

The symposium addressed the multiple challenges and possibilities American colleges and universities face when assessing how to build or expand their international dimensions. The most basic challenge involves answering this question: What exactly does it mean to internationalize? The symposium addressed many aspects of this fundamental question, including:

- the changing patterns of student flows from and to other countries
- the nature of international flows of faculty and scholars exchanges
- the nature and changing patterns of funding for students and international research
- the structure of study abroad programs and on-campus offerings
- the potential role of changing communications technology and its role in a global university

xiii

This symposium consisted of two major forms of presentations. There were four commissioned papers and three panels to respond to the papers and lead the discussions involving all symposium participants. The presenters at the symposium were:

- Richard Lyman, President Emeritus, Stanford University and Rockefeller Foundation
- Richard D. Lambert, Director, National Foreign Language Center
- Gareth Williams, Economist, Institute of Education, University of London
- Steven Muller, Chairman, The 21st Century Foundation
- Lewis Branscomb, Albert Pratt Public Service Professor, John F. Kennedy School of Government, Harvard University
- Gerhard Friedrich, Executive Consultant, President, Friedrich Associates
- Michael Aiken, Chancellor, University of Illinois
- Stephen R. Lewis, Jr., President, Carleton College
- Charles Vest, President, Massachusetts Institute of Technology
- Colin Campbell, President, Rockefeller Brothers Fund

AN OVERVIEW FROM RICHARD LYMAN

Richard Lyman's paper provides a broad context for the symposium. He contends that American higher education has not yet responded adequately to an international environment that increasingly immerses us in a global economy and tests our capacity to meet international challenges. He cites the problems of the general American ignorance of world geography, a lack of proficiency in foreign languages, and cultural parochialism when attempting to operate in an international setting. While American colleges and universities have paid lip service to the need for change in higher education institutions, Lyman believes there has been little hard thinking or action. Senior administrative officers are not clear on how to "internationalize" the campus, and do not always seize the opportunities available to them to gain more insight into the process. American institutions do not adequately prepare students to study abroad or to maximize the benefits of such experiences upon students' returns. Among academics, a bias against area centers and area studies is compounded by the difficulty of transforming the highly decentralized American educational system.

Lyman observes that concern over the American ability to remain economically, scientifically, and technologically competitive has led some leading institutions to implement change and make some progress. For example, the U.S. is the leading host country for exchange students; this has caused

American institutions to increase international course offerings, expand international collections in libraries, hire more faculty with international expertise, and offer more opportunities for student and faculty study abroad. Focus on domestic multiculturalism, which has been a central issue on campuses, may also spur further internationalization. Lyman suggests the need for a more intelligent debate on the best method for incorporating international and ethnic minority students into their American campuses—through integration or through differentiation.

Lyman recommends a number of ways to meet international challenges:

- proclaiming the message that the international environment should be considered in all educational endeavors
- examining the lessons to be learned from the model of the multinational corporation
- supporting creation of a National Foundation for International Studies
- coordinating action and information within the academic community about the ingenious programs for meeting international challenges to be found within individual colleges and universities

The papers by Richard Lambert, Gareth Williams, and Steven Muller address three important forms of capital that institutions must consider as they develop a strategic approach: (1) human capital, (2) financial capital, and (3) intellectual capital. To build and define a global university or college requires an understanding of both the flows and the investment of each form of capital.

FOREIGN STUDENT FLOWS

Richard Lambert describes the scale and composition of foreign student flows and their impact on the internationalization of campuses. Lambert shows that the overall number of foreign students at American institutions of higher education has been increasing, even though their share of the overall student population in 1990-91 was only 2.9%. While some other countries have enrolled a higher percentage of foreign students, the U.S. receives a larger share of all students who enroll in higher education institutions outside of their homeland. Lambert reports that more than half of the foreign students in American institutions come from Asian countries, primarily, in order of significance, China, Japan, Taiwan, India, and Korea. This trend has shifted over time.

Lambert points out that foreign flows at individual institutions can vary significantly from national patterns. Generally, Ph.D. granting institutions have the highest proportions of foreign students, with a recent shift away from private research institutions and towards large public institutions. Still, the dispersion of foreign students among U.S. institutions is remarkable; very few American colleges and universities have no foreign students.

Foreign students in American institutions also are concentrated in specific fields of specialization and academic levels. Overall, the liberal arts are underrepresented. The primary academic interests of foreign students in the U.S. are in business, engineering, the physical sciences, mathematics, and computer science. At the undergraduate level, business training draws more students; at the graduate level, science and technology education is preferred, particularly engineering.

According to Lambert, predicting future student flows is difficult because they depend upon multiple factors. Student flows are affected by federal and institutional policies on funding for international students (which appears at present to be shrinking) and foreign enrollment. World events and circumstances play a part as well. Foreign students in the U.S. often come from newly industrialized countries and countries that do not have highly developed, quality systems of higher education; these circumstances change over time. In addition, greater competition now exists, with other countries targeting and attracting more foreign students. The Immigration and Naturalization Service also is trying to control the foreign student population by progressively tightening visa regulations and conditions under which foreign students may seek employment.

Despite the pressures against the influx of foreign students, Lambert believes foreign students will continue to come to the U.S. for several reasons. Few countries have offerings as diverse and access as open as the U.S. Graduate school education in the U.S. is disarticulated from baccalaureate education. Graduate departments prefer to admit only the best students, and for the time being many of these come from other countries. Some schools claim foreign students are a good source of marginal revenue, even though little supporting analysis for this viewpoint has been performed. It is clear, however, that most foreign students pay their own way, and institutions are shifting their recruitment and admissions policies to target these "full pay" students.

Lambert observes the weak link between the foreign student population and the internationalization of the campus: Foreign students are best represented in the sciences, and least represented in international courses and majors. As a result, American students do not benefit enough from different cultural perspectives in the classroom. Compounding this problem is the lack of symbiosis between American student flows abroad and foreign flows to the U.S.

TRENDS IN EUROPEAN FINANCES

Gareth Williams provides a comparative perspective by describing the changing higher education systems of Western Europe. He highlights the enormous variation in structure and financing of higher education systems among the 12 countries of the European Community, which are greater than the differences among American institutions.

The European Community exhibits two predominant approaches to higher education: provision by the state, the dominant model in France; and private initiative, increasingly the dominant model in Great Britain. Most countries in the Community approximate the French model. Many European nations have a significant "non-university" sector, (i.e., professional preparatory schools that focus less on research and are funded less generously than the university sector), and much of the growth in enrollment in these countries has occurred in this sector. Expenditures are difficult to compare in the European Community because the funding and accounting systems for salaries and for research and student aid vary considerably, particularly in light of the differences between publicly and privately funded institutions.

In the funding area, Western European institutions of higher education have been undergoing the same transition affecting their American counterparts. Many governments have introduced an incentive-based model to replace the previously dominant control-oriented model. Financial incentives include shifting from input-based formulae to output-oriented formulae, charging student fees, providing conditional grants, and increasing the stringency of public funding for higher education.

Williams describes the changes in higher education funding in Great Britain during the 1980s and 1990s. The period saw modest growth in resources, but a substantial decline in public expenditures per student. Teaching efficiency rose during this period: the number of graduates rose by 10%, the proportion receiving first class honors degrees increased from 6% to 8.3%, the number of higher degrees rose by 60%, and the number of Ph.D.'s rose by over 34%. Williams suggests that the increases in efficiency may be a result of a shift from incremental and loosely monitored formula funding by a single government agency towards more closely specified formulae and contractual funding by a wider variety of public and private funding bodies.

Williams concludes with a discussion of the recent initiatives undertaken by the European Community to integrate national systems. The Community has been active in two areas: harmonization of professional qualifications and promotion of staff and student mobility programs between countries. A network of National Academic Recognition Centers has been established to provide employers, students, and institutions with authoritative information on the value and recognition of educational credentials obtained in other countries. Among staff and student mobility programs, the best known is ERASMUS, the European Community Action Scheme for the Mobility of University Students, an organization that funds the living costs of students who complete at least one unit of their courses in a country other than their own. Overall, however, higher education in the Community is far from being standardized, and Williams predicts this will not occur if authorities of the European Community continue to be barred from direct involvement in education.

THE GLOBALIZATION OF KNOWLEDGE

Steven Muller observes that the third dimension of capital, knowledge, has always been a source of power. In technologically advanced societies, the information industry provides many of the sources of knowledge and power. This industry has made intellectual capital widely accessible and has reduced geographic distances, national borders, and, to some extent, language barriers. Modern countries have become heavily dependent upon pervasive applications of information technology, and now knowledge has become a commodity. As such, knowledge is the most essential and highly prized product of the information age.

In this context, Muller describes four ways the globalization of knowledge affects the American higher education institution. First, institutions need to determine how to access and manage the international flow of knowledge. Gaining knowledge is easiest if the college or university participates in consortia, which identify, collect, assemble, and organize material for subscribers. He observes that the ability to use the full range of resources requires the institution, primarily the faculty, to be willing to make a significant and sustained investment in time and energy and to assign a high priority to doing so.

Second, commercial and national interests are at stake when universities share their knowledge on an international basis. True to their tradition of openness, universities have successfully insisted that industry-sponsored university research remain accessible. However, Muller warns that the time may come when, in the name of national security and economic competitiveness, U.S. policy will limit flows of intellectual capital by obstructing the flow of information. Another concern he raises is the risk that increasing industry support of university research may become less mutually beneficial as industry increases the incentives for applied research to the long-term detriment of the university's support of basic research.

Muller also speaks about the societal impact of the increasing value of knowledge as a commodity. He observes that the information age is likely to widen the gap between the haves and the have-nots—in this country and around the world. He asks what is the appropriate role of American higher education in dealing with this issue, and he observes that outreach to the educationally disadvantaged must take on new meaning, both in domestic and international programs.

Finally, Muller raises what he considers the largest question to be answered in any discussion of the future of the global institution: Will globalizing intellectual capital assist or hinder the university in its greatest task—integrative conceptualization? To date, Muller believes that the effect of the knowledge explosion has been to foster just the opposite: fragmentation and specialization. He ends by challenging higher education to become the instrument of the ongoing reintegration of knowledge and to do so on an international scale.

THE ROLE OF TECHNOLOGY

One of the constant themes in discussions of how to define the global university is the pivotal role of technology. To bring this subject into more perspective, two nationally recognized experts associated with the nexus between the high tech industry and higher education were invited to the symposium to speculate on how technology will transform teaching, research, and the transportation of knowledge. Lewis Branscomb began the session by observing that universities are never the first to use the technology they create. Universities have been successful in organizing for technology by using the Internet and creating organizations like EDUCOM. Around the globe, 10 million people have access to Internet. EDUCOM has been extremely influential in defining the future of the National Research and Education Network (NREN), a billion dollar program sponsored by Congress to develop an upgraded, computer network linking universities with industrial and governmental laboratories.

Major strides still need to be taken before information technology transforms the character of the teaching, research, and administrative functions. The possibilities remain largely untapped in computer-assisted learning, lifelong learning, distance learning, computer-based scholarship and research, electronic publishing, and enhanced administrative effectiveness and efficiency.

Branscomb explored the reasons why universities have been slow to use technology to increase instructional productivity and effectiveness. Faculties have little incentive to increase their teaching productivity (in contrast to research productivity), and students have little incentive to request productivity increases.

Finally, Branscomb addressed the conundrum of providing open access to scholarship worldwide while protecting national economic interests. He believes institutions will have to walk a very fine line between the two. Universities can maintain the balance by doing the following:

- updating the curriculum in engineering to encourage innovation
- supporting a national technology strategy that addresses the waste in many government "megaprojects"
- refusing to be overly swayed by political pressures arising from concerns about U.S. competitiveness, for which universities are being blamed for more than their fair share
- recognizing that the ultimate solution requires society to discover that its self-interest lies in a global market of ideas and goods, and that universities represent society's eyes and ears, learning from and teaching others

Gerhard Friedrich questions whether American universities will be seen as leaders in the global knowledge-based economy. Friedrich suggests that leadership is possible because, at a minimum, higher education institutions hold the primary raw material.

Three technologies shape Friedrich's vision of the future: the network/ research library, broad-band satellite telecommunication, and global imaging. The first technological tool is already well advanced, yet some further innovations are necessary to connect very different institutions. The second technology advance means face-to-face interaction is possible from across the globe. As the costs of this technology continue to fall dramatically, the notion of location-independent education in international study becomes increasingly realistic. The third tool is being used by NASA in an environmental project called Sequoia 2000, which models dynamically the earth's atmosphere in real-time. This application can conceivably be used in higher education to model knowledge flows.

Friedrich sees several roles for universities to play in the world economy. Moreover, he believes that the success of National Technical University, a university without a physical campus that involves the best educators and allows students to learn from anywhere in the world, will soon begin to challenge the need for traditional campuses.

Although Friedrich finds no clear answers as to how the university can be a leader in the global knowledge-based economy, it is clear that interdisciplinary discussions and programs need to be sponsored. To achieve leadership and to avoid being exploited, institutions need to consider how to innovate and become, before it is too late, an entrepreneurial player in a global economy.

THREE VOICES OF EXPERIENCE: CARLETON COLLEGE, MIT, UNIVERSITY OF PENNSYLVANIA

Every college or university represented at the symposium was engaged in a variety of international programs, but many had only recently begun to give high priority to a re-examination of the nature and future directions of the international aspects of the institution. The presidents of four institutions, identified as among those at the forefront of developing a comprehensive international strategy, were invited to speak about their experiences and concerns in formulating their institutions' roles in the international environment. These four institutions were Carleton College, MIT, the University of Pennsylvania, and Indiana University. [Unfortunately, President Ehrlich of Indiana University was unable to attend; a description of the importance and extent of internationalization at Indiana University is summarized in his annual report, "The University in the State," published in the winter of 1992.] The observations by the other three presidents of their own institution's efforts to define what it means to be an international institution are summarized in this volume.

This panel led to the discussion of many important questions that every campus must address: What constitutes the internationalization of a campus? What kinds of conditions nurture it? How do we educate students to work in the global marketplace? How do we develop strong ties with the rest of the world? How can we balance the needs of American security against the free exchange of people, ideas, and resources that is essential to the advancement of knowledge? How can we maximize the value of an overseas experience for our students? How can we encourage and support more faculty research overseas? How can we increase the importance of area studies and interdisciplinary work with international dimensions? How can we link language teaching with other aspects of the curriculum? How can we address the growing problem of financing both overseas study by American students and the study of foreign students in our own institutions? What kinds of organizational changes are needed on campuses to foster better planning and coordination of international programs and to integrate more international experience into the lives of domestic students? What does it mean to internationalize the curriculum? Are there ways to tap new resources for internationalization, such as overseas alumni and multinational corporations?

NEXT STEPS TO MEETING THE CHALLENGE

Colin Campbell, a long-time observer of the role of higher education in the international context, summarized and integrated the proceedings. This symposium underscores the serious challenge that global interdependence represents to educators and policymakers. This reality is not being reflected to the degree it should be in the experience of today's undergraduate and graduate students, or in the teaching and research programs and priorities of our colleges and universities, or in the higher education policies and initiatives of the federal government. Three shortcomings of American education prevent students from gaining an international perspective, according to Campbell.

- Preparation for university-level work is inadequate and inferior, particularly in math, science, foreign languages, writing, and history.
- Financial aid funds are insufficient, making it increasingly difficult to allocate funds for international activities, including student flows.
- The fragmentation of knowledge and emphasis upon specialization discourages global thinking.

The problems for higher education institutions seeking an international role are not insurmountable, but the unevenness in institutional approaches to preparing American students for foreign study and to maximizing the experiences of international students and their American hosts and peers tells us that many opportunities for improvement are being missed. Scholarly mobility and breadth and depth of interaction are not enhanced by current levels of language training and current social and living arrangements in U.S. institutions.

Campbell recognizes the disappearance of barriers to rapid information flow produced by the revolution in communications technology, and the potential opportunities this presents to universities for participating in the creation of a global marketplace for intellectual capital. He notes, however, the other side of the coin. Access and management of information is costly; confidentiality, secrecy, and proprietary issues are controversial; and inequality of access can create new problems and frictions.

To address some of the problems caused by the era of information technology, Campbell made a number of suggestions:

- Maximize learning from study abroad; institutions and groups of institutions should develop approaches to prepare students for foreign study and for follow-up upon their return.
- Link the environmental issue to internationalization to have a greater impact on both.
- Create a national foundation or agency, whose mission is to disseminate good models of internationalization in education.
- Lobby the Clinton administration, possibly with the help of foundation programs, to:
  Provide more financial support for American graduate and undergraduate students.
  Establish a sensible tax policy for foreign students receiving financial assistance, so they are not dissuaded from studying in the U.S.
  Reconsider the enormous cut in training funds for students from developing countries.

- Encourage ongoing dialogue domestically and internationally about the internationalization of education.
- Foster a dialogue with American institutional leaders regarding the dilemma of intellectual protectionism versus free flow of ideas.

AN ADDED DIMENSION: THE DEVELOPING WORLD

Finally, this volume concludes with an additional paper relating to the challenges and opportunities in the developing countries of the world. Although this topic was not a focus at the symposium, the editors believe that this essay adds an important dimension to this volume, one which campuses will want to consider as they develop their own plans for defining their place in the international arena.

KHH

Overview

❧ ❧ ❧ ❧ ❧ ❧ ❧ ❧

Richard Lyman

I t is easy to see why our topic, "International Challenges for American Higher Education," is high on everyone's agenda. As Robert Black and George Bonham wrote 13 years ago:

> The nature of profound change in this country's immersion in global events and developments can no longer be denied, even by the hardiest Troglodyte. It is less and less possible to separate foreign from domestic events, or to think of crises as purely national or purely foreign, or, for that matter, to think of any major field of academic study that can any longer be the focus of purely domestic visions.[1]

The revolution in communications technology was and is the principal cause of "this profound change." We are deluged with striking information about it; for example, the value of foreign exchange traded in New York in one week often equals the total annual product of the American economy.[2] Two years ago, Norman McRae hit upon a striking analogy when seeking to explain in *The Economist* the troubles international bankers were having. Suppose, he wrote, that "in the nineteenth century some weird form of transubstantiation has suddenly made it possible to transfer the cheapest Argentine beef and Canadian grain, with nil transportation costs, instantly to Europe." The impact, not only on European agriculture but upon the world's overall economy, would have been enormous, and enormously destabilizing. Yet, McRae went on, "In this age of keying instant commands to computers' screens, exactly that transubstantiation has happened to the products of banking."

1

The American people are not well positioned to meet the challenges presented by global change on such a scale and proceeding at such a pace. At the most rudimentary level, American ignorance of the world is striking. According to a widely cited Gallup survey conducted five years ago for the National Geographic Society, one out of five American adults could not name a single European nation, one-half could not find South Africa on the map (despite the considerable hint contained in the name itself), and half could not name the country in which the Sandinistas and Contras were then fighting. Many thought it was in Honduras, Iran, Lebanon, or Afghanistan.[3]

Most ominous of all, of the nine countries surveyed, the U.S. was the only one in which the youngest repondents (18 to 24) did less well than the oldest (over-55). In short, our condition is unsatisfactory and appears to be worsening.

At less elementary levels, the Ugly American may be less evident in world capitals than 40 years ago, but cultural parochialism and arrogance have not disappeared. In his book-length essay, *Barbarian Sentiments: How the American Century Ends*, William Paff grants that we no longer expect the rest of the world to fall in step behind us merely by the power of our example. But, he contends, when we try to influence the behavior of other nations and peoples, "Americans nearly always make use of simple models of social change and politics, related to our own national experience and values." In part this tendency derives from our persistent view of ourselves as "the 'new world,' successor to the 'old' world, which is Europe." This viewpoint has led us since the Second World War to think of the countries of Asia, Africa, and the Middle East as "new nations." Having, like us, freed themselves from European control, their future should resemble our past, at least until they catch up with us. In fact, these countries are far older than we. "They are not following us, somewhere on a road that we have already traveled."[4] We cannot judge where they are headed by remembering where we have been.

Beyond these issues of attitudes and perceptions are serious questions of institutional preparedness.

In a notoriously monolingual society, we are still in disarray as to how, when, and to whom to teach which foreign languages. And, unless things have changed radically since the Educational Testing Service survey of 1980, "there is essentially no relationship between proficiency in a modern foreign language and the overall global knowledge" of U.S. college undergraduates.[5] Language learning seems to occur in a vacuum.

Most foreign language instruction is at elementary levels. Accomplishment is generally measured by credit hours passed, not degree of proficiency attained. Language requirements, either for matriculation or graduation, though much discussed, are of dubious value. "None of the four-year institutions [studied by our leading expert on the subject, Richard Lambert] actually required entering students to demonstrate a minimal level of foreign language competency through an examination; total 'seat time' is enough."[6] The discussion often appears to assume that it makes no difference what languages are studied. But in today's world, does it make sense that four-fifths of total enrollments are still in Spanish, French, and German?

The entire question of scholarly mobility, from undergraduate exchange programs to coordination of research across national boundaries, suffers not only from "Absence of Decision," to borrow the title of one of Craufurd Goodwin and Michael Nacht's genial but unsparing monographs, but also from a lack of coherent discussion of policy alternatives among those in a position to make policy changes. This is so despite the fact that many in academia think that scholarly mobility is what is *meant* by "internationalization."

Continuing difficulties with the structure of institutions may go to the heart of the academic enterprise. Can institutions constructed of schools and departments based on scholarly disciplines be expected to meet the interdisciplinary requirements for understanding other lands and cultures? After World War II, doubts about this possibility gave rise to the development of area studies centers and institutes. In the 1940s, three committees of the Social Science Research Council considered "the legitimacy of area studies as a division of the universe of knowledge, and their usefulness as a corrective to the organizational fragmentation of the curriculum among many contending disciplinary departments." Not surprisingly, the disciplines prevailed; the Hall report of 1947 recommended that area studies be seen as "an additional competence" that should stop at the master's degree level.[7] An "additional competence" they largely remain, but the doubts persist. We may need to think about some kinds of reordering, or at least of constructing centers of countervailing power that will be more effective than such devices have proven to date.

A couple of years ago, Washington State University hosted a conference entitled "Internationalizing U.S. Universities: A Time for Leadership." Apparently it was not a time for leadership to attend such a meeting, however, at least not top leadership; the attendance list of 124 was replete with "Assistants to" and with directors of international programs offices or centers, but included just six presidents, none from an AAU or COFHE institution.[8]

Lip service to the need for change is widespread, indeed all but universal. But hard thinking on the subject is rarer. One paper prepared for this same conference reported that the senior administrators interviewed were highly supportive of internationalization. But when pressed as to what the term might mean or imply, either generally or for their institution, most of those interviewed clearly "had thought about the topics very little."[9] Ten years ago, Goodwin and Nacht found a similar condition:

...some leaders in higher education are attempting to construct a new vision of the college or university in the United States at the end of the 20th century. Just as major businesses have moved abroad and become multinational, they argue, so must higher education jettison its provincialism. . . . Yet typically we found the articulation of the concept somewhat vague; it rests on the conviction that students from other countries have a crucial part to play in higher education. . . . But the comparison between internationalizing higher education and extending markets overseas seemed to be receiving far more lip service than scrutiny.[10]

For too long, international education, especially exchange and study abroad programs, were justified by a vague sense that such studies were the path to mutual understanding and world peace. On this subject, however, fervor has generally tended to displace analysis. Writings on the topic were characterized by an Apocalyptic sense of urgency—nothing short of total solutions *now* would save us. Here is a brief example of this urgency from a relatively recent symposium entitled *Sharing the World—A Prospect for Global Learning*:[11]

Our awakening must take place simultaneously in all the dimensions of man and society—namely, spiritual, moral, cultural, social, political, and economic.

But if. . .the world cannot "live as one"—and time seems to be running out—then it will surely die in millions. It is, perhaps, the moment of the dreamers to be heard. And Global Learning is a dream that seems to offer one of the most hopeful prospects.

Today, internationalizing education in the U.S. is proposed as a way to help restore our economic competitiveness in the world. This approach is somewhat more hardheaded, and its more obvious points have been clear to us for some time. The President's Commission chaired by James Perkins alerted us to the importance of learning about our potential customers and competitors back in 1979, and Senator Paul Simon has regaled us for years with tales about how the General Motors slogan "Bodies by Fisher" came out in Flemish as "Corpses by Fisher" or how "Come Alive with Pepsi!" nearly appeared in the Chinese translation of the *Reader's Digest* as "Pepsi Brings Your Ancestors Back from the Dead." A non-commercial example that I like even better involves an American publication on air power that referred mysteriously to the "wet sheep" alleged to reside under the wings of MIG jets; these turned out to be "hydraulic rams."

Such concerns remain valid, but others, more subtle and more profound, have been added. In particular, as both the quantity and quality of scientific and technological research in other countries has improved, American self-sufficiency in such matters has eroded. In more and more fields, Americans find it essential to keep up with developments abroad, by reading, traveling to conferences, welcoming scholars from other countries to their laboratories, and collaborating with them on joint projects. As the 1991 report of the faculty study group on the "International Relations of MIT in a Technologically Competitive World" states:

> In some ways, international scientific and technological parity represents a return to the situation of the earlier decades of this century, when it was necessary to keep up with European developments in order to stay at the forefront of a field.[12]

Today one must add Japan and even several developing countries to Europe as sources of both competition and required knowledge.

The exchange of students and faculty is a common thread running through almost all institutional efforts to meet the demands of a changed U.S. situation in the world. While statistics on scholarly mobility are notoriously unreliable, it is clear that students have been crossing national borders in pursuit of their studies in steadily increasing numbers for many years. By one set of estimates, the world total nearly quadrupled between 1960 and 1980, to nearly one million.[13] Growth appears to have slowed somewhat in the 1980s, but the collapse of political barriers to free movement in Eastern Europe and the active promotion of mobility in the European Community should stimulate further expansion in the numbers. Policy, too, has changed. In many of the "receiving" countries of OECD, the 1970s were a time of skepticism concerning the value of taking on international students, and this was reflected in various restrictive policies. In the 1980s, this changed rather dramatically; the talk now, at least in OECD countries, is all of competition, meeting the demands of the "market," etc. Various signs of restricting student flows have been noted in Third World countries, but how significant these will turn out to be is hard to judge. The needs that gave rise to extensive study abroad by citizens of these countries have not disappeared.[14]

The United States is, of course, the leading host country by a wide margin: 37.5% of the world's foreign students were here by the most recent estimates, followed by France (13.1%), the United Kingdom (5.7%), Italy (3.0%), and Canada (2.9%).[15] There were about 8,000 foreign students in this country in 1943; in 1990-91, there were 50 times that number (407,500).[16]

International students in the U.S. outnumber U.S. students going abroad by nearly six to one. Those who come here are typically graduate students from developing countries seeking scientific, technical, or management training to advance their careers and serve their countries. Most (64%) are males, though this is starting to change.[17] American students going abroad are predominantly undergraduates seeking cultural enrichment in Europe, and about two-thirds are female.

In effect, when we talk about the movement of students to and from this country we are talking about two quite different phenomena. Both may have something to do with internationalizing higher education, but closer affinities in terms of demographics, purposes, and impact are hard to find. Many Americans who go abroad do not enroll in foreign universities, lacking the requisite linguistic skills. Often they go under institutional auspices aimed as much at protecting them from drowning in a foreign culture as at teaching them to swim there.[18]

The rosy glow of the early Fulbright years has faded considerably. Richard Lambert finds that "the current system of providing grants allowing future language and area specialists to visit their countries of specialization is capricious, inflexible, and poorly tailored to the needs of students."[19] It is quite a feat to produce a mechanism that is at the same time inflexible and capricious.

There is also the usual quota of unintended consequences from governmental policies. Federal undergraduate student financial aid policies, for example, and those of some states, tend to promote our already dubious preference for "relatively protective American programs giving U.S. credit directly," and to penalize "mainstreaming"—enrolling U.S. students abroad in foreign universities.[20]

On the other hand, our notoriously heavy dependence upon importing foreigners to maintain enrollments and teaching and research programs in the sciences and especially in engineering has come about by accident, and persisted by neglect. There has been no serious effort to counter the effects of private industry's devouring America's (and its own) seed corn by hiring newly graduated engineers straight out of BS and MS programs rather than encouraging them to pursue doctorates and careers in academia.

We in higher education need not feel singled out. Lack of a clearly thought out and coherent set of policies at the federal level is hardly a rarity. We all but demand such policies by our explicit allegiance to maintaining the world's most highly decentralized educational system. If improvements are going to come, they are likely for the most part to emanate from state systems (though Goodwin and Nacht wonder why the admirable California programs have not found more imitators in other states) and individual institutional initiatives, including moves to create consortia in the interests of achieving economies of scale.

One can discover ingenious programs in individual American colleges and universities aimed at some of our obvious problems: e.g., arrangements at the Universities of Illinois and Massachusetts to send undergraduates to Third World universities and pay for it by training young faculty from those same institutions.[21] Goodwin and Nacht devote a chapter of their *Abroad and Beyond: Patterns in American Overseas Education* to promising innovations scattered across the country at all levels. The authors express the hope that such entrepreneurial activity in particular institutions will serve to counter the growth of a conservative "study abroad bureaucratic establishment that is beginning to emerge in American higher education today."[22]

My own university, Stanford University, once spawned a protective system of undergraduate enclaves, complete with Stanford faculty to teach in them, in such centers of world culture as Semmering, Austria, and Beutelsbach, Germany. Today Stanford has moved to create a highly promising multi-purpose center in Kyoto, Japan, with a mix of undergraduate, graduate, and post-graduate programs; the involvement of other U.S. institutions in supplying the undergraduate population (thus dealing with the problem of inadequate numbers of undergraduates competent in Japanese language); and an emphasis on scholarship in scientific and technical fields rather than exclusively on "cultural broadening." The hope is that Kyoto will be more than an overseas studies center, promoting the movement of scholars at all levels between the two countries and their interaction with the corporate and government spheres through internships, workshops, and the like.

The development of scholarly mobility in the U.S. could be advanced by its obvious relation to the domestic multiculturalism that is so central an issue on many campuses today. As Lambert puts it, "The United States is becoming a permanent multicultural society in which the world is us, not some distant backdrop against which the American drama is played out."[23] At the 1990 conference at Washington State University, Governor Booth Gardner spoke eloquently about "making connections between global and domestic cultural diversity."[24]

Such connections are by no means automatic. Minority students and faculty pushing for domestic multiculturalism are often markedly unsympathetic to internationalization, at least when it is a matter of bringing in people of color from other countries, which is seen as a devious way of appearing to meet affirmative action goals without in fact doing so.

It has long been a source of complaint that so little educational advantage has accrued to U.S. students from the presence in their midst of substantial numbers of foreign students, who, like our ethnic minority students, tend to segregate themselves in enclaves. In both cases, there is a painful dilemma between "integration" and "differentiation." Are the international and minority students to be treated as much as possible like the rest of the student body, or are they to have special programs—academic, residential, social, and cultural—devised to meet their needs?[25]

On this as on so many questions, across-the-board answers are not likely to be helpful. When Third World students who come to the U.S. for advanced work find themselves being taught by faculty members with little experience or knowledge of their students' homeland, but lots of enthusiasm for the latest in scientific and technical equipment, the resulting training will probably not be terribly useful back home. The visitors may be less inclined to blame their professors or the American university than to find fault with their homeland, and be tempted to join the brain drain. Our belief in freedom of movement and choice clashes head-on with our desire to assist Third World countries to develop. Further, the decisive factor may be that one country's brain drain is another's brain gain; we may *need* the foreigners' skills so much that we do all we can to make it easy for them to stay here. One observer has put the matter starkly:

> The U.S. higher education community has yet to face the ethical dimen-
> sions of its role in facilitating the continuing hemorrhage of talent from
> other less fortunate countries.[26]

When the visitor is here to do social science, or to study management, it is even more difficult to strike the right balance between attention to the conditions and circumstances of less developed countries (LDC) and fidelity to U.S. methods and standards. Among Brazilians who came here to study these "softer" fields, "The qualities of enforced breadth and methodological rigor in American graduate training were perceived to have special significance in the social sciences."[27] They came to appreciate especially "balance, measure, caution and moderation, in contrast to the shrill and simplistic debate which can be heard throughout much of Latin America."[28]

Such students may often feel alienated when they return home—if they return home. Should we, however, be upset when students return home no longer tolerant of racial and sexual discrimination or repression and denial of human rights as a result of experiences in the U.S.? Alienation of this kind is hardly cause for lamentation.

Although the U.S. is by far the biggest provider of education for students from other lands, other countries also face these questions. The Japanese have ambitious programs. There is also the burgeoning movement within the European Community, symbolized by ERASMUS and other programs, for facilitating cross-border movement of students. There may sometimes be lessons for us in the experience of others, however tempted we may be to think that the traffic in advice should flow from us to them. Are not the Europeans only now struggling to create something like the system of readily transferable academic credits that we have enjoyed, and sometimes suffered from, for decades? But we might learn something from PROCOPE (Projets de Cooperation et d'Echange), the attempt by the French and German governments to reduce the barriers that keep scientists of different countries but related fields from collaborative research. We in the U.S. have discussed for years the feasibility of making student loans repayable on the basis of income earned after graduation; the Australians have actually introduced such a program.[29]

Programs developed in other countries, under different educational, political, and cultural circumstances, are not always readily transplanted, however. The Australians are apparently also able to briskly deport any Third World students who threaten to join the brain drain at the end of their formal studies. Compare that with the spirit of the U.S. Supreme Court's 1982 *Plyler v. Doe* decision, whereby it is illegal to deny an applicant admission on the basis of his or her undocumented immigrant status.[30]

A Netherlands Organisation for International Cooperation in Higher Education report asserts that too much time and energy is now devoted to promoting student mobility, as against "internationalizing the education given to people who spend their entire student careers in the Netherlands."[31] With only about one-half of 1% of our students abroad at any given time, excessive mobility is not an American problem. What we need to worry about is the integration of overseas study with the rest of an individual's education. Rarely is the preparation for going overseas academically rigorous; the difficulty of insisting on language training as a prerequisite for study abroad is only the most obvious part of the problem. Even more clearly, institutions tend to do little or nothing to assure that returning students maximize the benefits derived form their work abroad by linking it with their subsequent studies back home. As Lambert remarks, study abroad for Americans "is by and large a totally enclaved experience."[32]

This brings us to the matter of "International Challenges to the American Curriculum." Perhaps the most disturbing finding in the 1980 ETS survey was that seniors averaged only eight points higher than freshmen on the knowledge test—"a smaller difference than one would expect of students who have had four years of higher education," as the authors rather temperately note.[33] That this should have been the case after some four decades of growth in international studies as an academic enterprise certainly raises questions.

Robert McCaughey examined this problem nine years ago in his book, *International Studies and Academic Enterprise.* He noted the familiar fact that when it comes to teaching, faculty members are first and foremost interested in training specialists like themselves. This preoccupation, and the concomitant neglect of undergraduate teaching,

> were general tendencies throughout academic life. . . . Yet insofar as international studies contributed to both those tendencies, there is considerable irony in their having done so, given the high hopes many academic reformers originally had for the enterprise's potential as a catalyst for curricular innovation. International studies were supposed to help meet not only the national challenge of intellectual parochialism but also, given its interdisciplinary nature, "the challenge of departmental parochialism" that some saw besetting American higher education.

McCaughey quoted Richard Morse's remark that international studies would "serve as a Trojan horse for academic reform."[34] But he went on to say that Morse's Trojan horse never materialized, for "Even at universities where regional programs acquired full departmental status. . .faculty members were careful to maintain their disciplinary base as well," and their graduate students took their degrees in the disciplines. Indeed, with their "second home" in an area center, international studies faculty were able to live "at more effective remove from the daily distractions of university life, not least those related to classroom teaching." Small wonder that "area centers by the early 1960s had come to be regarded almost everywhere among faculty concerned with the teaching of undergraduates as hostile bastions of academic entrepreneurship."

It seems unlikely that these conditions have changed much since. Disciplines are valued in higher education according to "how deep they dig their wells. . .[when what] they actually need [is] roads and bridges," writes a bruised teacher of modern languages.[35] The iron law of specialization is constantly at work to make knowledge more esoteric and to increase its quantity to the point where overarching comprehension is less and less conceivable. The condescension, sometimes bordering on contempt, with which many scholars in the disciplines regard colleagues who study regions instead of contributing to the development of the discipline's theoretical structure does not appear to have diminished greatly since 1984, despite Fred Wakeman's efforts while he headed the Social Science Research Council.[36] Contempt of regional studies is no longer limited mainly to economists enjoying the higher altitudes of mathematical abstraction; it is growing common among denizens of other social sciences striving to emulate economics, and even among humanists devoted to the thin but apparently bracing air of deconstructionism, whose passion for either undergraduate teaching or interdisciplinary explorations can readily be contained. One reads about "a rebellious faction" of literature scholars in the early 1980s who are said to have "contended that contemporary critical approaches were 'decidedly limp,' and argued that English must become 'rigorous and dryer' lest it should degenerate into a 'flabby and monstrous non-subject.' "[37] Not much room for undergraduate survey courses there.

There is nevertheless some movement towards strengthening the global aspects of the curriculum. University self-studies, such as those undertaken at Penn and MIT, are numerous. At the University of California at San Diego, each undergraduate college sets its own general education requirements, which allows Fifth College to emphasize international studies. All students take a six-quarter survey called The Making of the Modern World, the syllabi for which are both impressive and intriguing, as well as a "regional specialization" consisting of three courses dealing with a specific region of the world.

The exogenous facts sometimes exert a pressure that is hard to resist. Certain aspects of the environmental problems facing humanity can only be understood, let alone dealt with, globally. The growth of interrelatedness, sometimes amounting to interdependence, among national economies means that to confine one's study to a single national economy, even the world's largest, is often not practicable. Graduate schools of business may indeed be slow to adjust to the new global context; they cannot turn their faculties into international studies experts overnight. But their students are pushing them to broaden their horizons, and the facts of the market are pushing the students, whose primary aim is, after all, to become employable.

Surveys of undergraduate education suggest some forward movement. The American Council on Education reported in 1988 that more than half of the four-year colleges and universities responding showed increases in the preceding five years in "hiring of new faculty with international expertise, international course offerings, libraries' international collections, opportunities for study abroad, [and] opportunities for faculty travel abroad."[38] Still, these are general categories, and "more than half" hardly constitutes a tidal wave. It is hard to imagine how a college could report that it had *not* made *any* increase in its library's international collections. If 68% of the "presidents and other senior officials" surveyed said they considered "the acquisition of a knowledge and understanding of international affairs was 'very important,'" four out of five thought that same thing about "a knowledge of American history, an understanding of the Western heritage, the ability to use English well, familiarity with natural sciences and acquiring basic skills in mathematics." It looks like a case of "All have won and all shall have prizes." An accurate sense of operational priorities is hard to come by, and one harks back to the reiterated complaint that many deans and presidents talk a good fight but have not thought hard about what's involved, let alone committed themselves to accomplishing the necessary changes.

In the face of so much complexity and so many shortcomings, what is to be done to improve academia's capacity to meet "The International Challenges to American Higher Education"? Massive efforts have already been made over a long period of time to diminish U.S. parochialism, rationalize our nonsystem of teaching foreign languages, and replace the aimless academic tourism of U.S. undergraduates with serious work abroad that is linked significantly to their work at home.

With all due respect—and much *is* due—to those who have been battling on these fronts for decades, we may have placed too much reliance on cries of alarm, which are proverbially a wasting asset. The President's Commission of 1979, chaired by James A. Perkins, was a classic example. Its report contained much that was obvious and serious—Americans *are* monoglot and widely ignorant, as we have seen—but also, I'm sorry to say, much that was based on nothing more than self-serving testimony from international studies scholars.

Only one of the twenty-five studies conducted for the commission, that by the Rand Corporation on the occupational demand for international studies specialists, did generate the kinds of data that might have served as a check against the possibility that the views expressed from within the enterprise did not fully describe the situation. Unfortunately the Rand report, which concluded there were twice as many international studies PhDs being produced by American universities in the late 1970s as there were jobs for them, was the one report not included among those published by the commission.[39]

To have attempted a semi-suppression of the Rand findings was not even tactically smart. It would surely have been far better to argue that the low demand expressed by business, in particular, was the result of the very parochialism and lack of foresight the Commission had been created to battle. But the Chicken Little, sky-is-falling tone is all too frequently encountered in discussions of international education. After a while it numbs the mind of anyone not already wholeheartedly in tune with international education. Why, then, does it persist?

In part it is a matter of sheer frustration. It *ought* to be shocking that so few Americans know any other language, that so many have only the foggiest notion of geography, that the U.S. is alone among significant powers in not insisting on *any* linguistic competence as a prerequisite to a career in the Foreign Service, and that these and other lamentable conditions have persisted for so long. But this is not the case. The U.S. public was less than swept off its feet by being told "that when Iraq invaded Kuwait two summers ago, the U.S. military found only 18 of 3 million American active-duty and reserve troops fluent in the Arabic dialect spoken in Iraq"—this from a longtime champion, first in the Congress and later as president of a leading university, of international education.[40] Even if all the favorite prescriptions of international studies proponents were to become the law and custom of the country tomorrow, it may be doubted that such esoteric linguistic skills would be endemic throughout our armed services. The situation may be improving, but much remains to be done, and competing voices on behalf of other priorities are so strong and so numerous.

Neither is it effective advocacy to go to the other extreme and make the needed changes sound simple, a mere matter of summoning the will to act. The president of a liberal arts college with an unusually strong record in things international writes:

> Yet, even though we have become participants in a borderless global economy, we have not changed undergraduate education significantly. We have the resources for change, on our faculties and in our student populations, but we have not used them to bring about significant global education.[41]

More to the point was the view expressed early in 1992 by one of our hosts for this conference, as reported in the *Boston Globe*:[42]

> Referring to the simple logistical difficulties of cooperative education ventures among schools in the Boston area, she said: "It's difficult enough even getting people in the Boston area together. If we're having a hard time convening colleagues here, we should not speak too glibly of the potential of the global university."

That our advocacy has sometimes been flawed does not mean that it has been generally misguided, or that it has not made progress over the years. The Coalition for the Advancement of Foreign Languages and International Studies made less noise than the President's Commission of 1979, but its work was much more sophisticated and more cognizant of the obstacles and the real complexities with which we must deal. I suppose we all know that the proposed National Foundation for International Studies, if it is ever created, will not "solve the problem"; the recent history of the two existing federal endowments, for the Arts and the Humanities, has been sobering. But, as *Points of Leverage: An Agenda for a National Foundation for International Studies* makes very clear, an NFIS could do a lot, particularly in promoting reform in our treatment of foreign languages throughout the educational system. Just being able to conceptualize the problems effectively would be a great forward step.

But no single structural change or augmentation will suffice. The task is one of infusion, of infiltrating all manner of educational endeavors with the recognition that the world has changed and continues to change in ways relevant to practically everything we in education do or think about. And infusion, even in so limited a set of mechanisms as the American college curriculum, is at best a terribly slow, difficult process. Consider the difficulty that defeated Richard Lambert's effort to find out just how much international content existed in college courses:

> We learned just how reluctant many faculty members were to share their syllabi with us, with departmental chairs, with deans, or with university faculty committees, even with the promise of detaching the professor's name from the course. We abandoned the effort...[43]

Lambert did not abandon the effort to think about the matter, however, and suggests a number of possible avenues of approach: through the national professional associations, through a reporting of progress in economics and political science textbooks, and through the accrediting mechanisms for business and engineering schools.

As two veteran observers report, indirect approaches can also work wonders:

> ...a very significant, though unintended, side effect of these contracts [for development assistance abroad under AID] has been to internation-

alize and deprovincialize the institutions. It is truly remarkable to visit one of the major land-grant universities today and find a cosmopolitan faculty and administration, often surpassing the older and more liberal arts-oriented sister institutions in the state. We met professors of range science and irrigation engineering who seemed substantially more self-confident about and conscious of the world than their presumably more internationalist historian and linguistic brethren down the road.[44]

One feels tempted to say, with Galileo after his enforced recantation before the Inquisition, "But still, it moves."

The strongest reason to believe that it will continue to move, and in a forward direction, however unevenly and unsystematically and with however many frustrations along the way, is simply the fact that recognition of the enormous changes in the world and in the situation of the United States is far more pervasive than at any time since our great conversion during and immediately after World War II, when the nation rejected its isolationist heritage. In the 1940s and 1950s the political facts of life finally penetrated the nation's consciousness. The economic and technological facts that propel the current global changes are even harder to ignore; they impinge on us at every turn. Higher education has always reflected the state of the nation, more or less, albeit often with some lagtime. The multinational corporation *will* eventually have its academic analogy.

Our overwhelming decentralization in intra-institutional processes, as well as in the inter-institutional, inter-state, and national processes, will assure that the evolution toward a global university will be messy and the results notably incoherent. Once again, Lambert puts it powerfully:

> The trouble is that the special quality of the American collegiate educational system, what distinguishes it from more centrally planned systems in other parts of the world, is its emphasis on autonomy, diversity, and productive chaos. The central question is clear: How do we accomplish our integrative goals in a system in which disaggregation of educational decisions is the dominant characteristic?[45]

The answer to Lambert's central question: Only by patient and relentless effort, in which symposia such as this play an important part. As a reminder that international perspectives have a considerable history in U.S. higher education, and that even disorder has its uses, let me close with a quotation from the dean of American higher education watchers, Clark Kerr, in his *Uses of the University* (1963):

> A university anywhere can aim no higher than to be as British as possible for the sake of the undergraduates, as German as possible for the sake of the graduates and research personnel, as American as possible for the sake of the public at large—and as confused as possible for the sake of the preservation of the whole uneasy balance.[46]

NOTES

1. *Annals of the American Academy of Political and Social Science*, 449 (May 1980), p. 103.
2. Graduate School of Business, Brandeis University, quoted in Craufurd D. Goodwin and Michael Nacht, *Abroad and Beyond: Patterns in American Overseas Education* (New York: Cambridge University Press, 1988), p. 102.
3. Richard D. Lambert, *International Studies and the Undergraduate* (Washington, DC: American Council on Education, 1989), pp. 105-06.
4. William Paff, *Barbarian Sentiments: How the American Century Ends* (New York: Noonday Press, 1990), p. 149.
5. Thomas S. Barrows, Stephen F. Klein, and John L.D. Clark, *What College Students Know and Believe About Their World* (New Rochelle, NY: Change Magazine Press, 1981). The possibility exists that truly *advanced* proficiency may make a difference. But that is of scant comfort since the numbers exhibiting such proficiency were too small to have a discernible impact on the sample.
6. Lambert, *International Studies and the Undergraduate*, p. 62.
7. See Ellen M. Gumperz, *Internationalizing American Higher Education* (Berkeley and Los Angeles: University of California Press, 1970), pp. 19-24.
8. In addition, the presidents of Washington State University and Oregon State University, and the chancellor of the Oregon State System, appeared as speakers on the program.
9. James B. Henson, Jan C. Noel, Thomas E. Gillard-Byers, and Marcus I. Ingle, "Internationalizing U.S. Universities—Preliminary Summary of a National Study" (Pullman, WA: Washington State University, 1990), p. 11.
10. Craufurd D. Goodwin and Michael Nacht, *Absence of Decision: Foreign Students in American Colleges and Universities* (New York: Institute of International Education, 1983), p. 1.
11. Hugh Oliver. *Sharing the World—A Prospect for Global Learning* (Toronto: Institute for Studies in Education, 1987), pp. 69 and 73. Towards the close of this conference one earthbound participant dared to say: "I am still not very clear about what we all mean by Global Learning. I can only take it that we are all living in one world and that we believe that learning and education are important. If I have failed to understand in what ways you think Global Learning is more than that, then I would love people to tell me."
12. "International Relations of MIT in a Technologically Competitive World," May 1, 1991, p. 5, note 5.
13. *Foreign Students and Internationalization of Higher Education: Proceedings of OECD/ Japan Seminar on Higher Education and the Flow of Students* (Hiroshima: Research Institute for Higher Education, 1989).
14. See Glenn L. Shive, S. Gopinathan, and William K. Cummings (Eds.), *North-South Scholarly Exchange: Access, Equity and Collaboration* (London and New York: Mansell Publishing, 1988). Chapter 17 is a useful summary.
15. Alan Wagner and Klaus Schnitzer, "Programmes and Policies for Foreign Students and Study Abroad: The Search for Effective Approaches in a New Global Setting," in *Higher Education XXI* (April 1991), p. 277.

16. Sherry L. Mueller, "Internationalism and Higher Education Patterns and Trends," presented at a symposium at the English Language Institute, University of Michigan, September 27, 1991.

17. See Phillip G. Altbach, "Impact and Adjustment: Foreign Students in Comparative Perspective," in *Higher Education* XXI (April 1991), p. 318.

18. Aquatic metaphors are all but irresistible in this discussion. For the fullest imaginable exploitation of them, see Goodwin and Nacht, *Abroad and Beyond*, Chapter 2.

19. *Points of Leverage: An Agenda for a National Foundation for International Studies* (New York: Social Science Research Council, 1986), p. 122.

20. Goodwin and Nacht, *Abroad and Beyond*, p. 59.

21. *ibid.*, p. 85.

22. *ibid.*, p. 91.

23. Lambert, *International Studies and the Undergraduate*, p. 1.

24. Foreign Students and Internationalization of Higher Education: Japanese Seminar on Higher Education and the Dean of Students, *Proceedings of OECD*, p. 7.

25. See the discussion concerning LDC students in Wagner and Schnitzer, "Programmes and Policies for Foreign Students and Study Abroad," *Higher Education*, pp. 282 ff.

26. David W. Stewart, "Immigration and Higher Education: The Crisis and the Opportunities," in *Educational Record* 72 (Fall, 1991), p. 24. Phillip Altbach, "Impact and Adjustment," *Higher Education*, p. 317, points out, however, that "What was once a 'one way street' in which Third World professionals migrated to the West, maintaining few contacts at home, has been transformed into a complex set of relationships in which emigrant professionals contribute significantly to a growing world economy and to the flow of expertise—and sometimes capital— from the industrialized nations to many Third World and newly industrializing nations."

27. Craufurd D. Goodwin and Michael Nacht, *Fondness and Frustration: The Impact of American Higher Education on Foreign Students with Special Reference to the Case of Brazil* (New York: Institute of International Education, 1981), p. 29.

28. *ibid.*, p. 30.

29. Under Australia's Higher Education Contribution Scheme, introduced in 1989, all students are required to contribute towards the cost of their higher education, either by lump-sum payment (which earns them a 15% discount) or by deferred payments through the tax system that are a given percentage of the students' gross income. See Maureen Woodhall, "Sharing the Costs of Higher Education: An International Analysis," in *Educational Record* 72 (Fall, 1991), pp. 27-36.

30. David W. Stewart, "Immigration and Higher Education," *Educational Record*.

31. Quoted in Wagner and Schnitzer, "Programmes and Policies for Foreign Students and Study Abroad," *Higher Education*, p. 281.

32. Lambert, *International Studies and the Undergraduate*, p. 40.

33. Barrows et al., *What College Students Know and Believe About Their World*, p. 39.

34. New York: Columbia University Press, 1984, pp. 220-221. An internal Ford Foundation document of 1969 declared: "It was always a guiding principle of the ITR [International Training and Research Program, the major source of funding for

area centers in the late 1950s and early '60s] that international studies would only be soundly built in American universities when they penetrated the established academic disciplines and professional specialties." Quoted in Robert E. Klitgaard, "Why International Studies? A Prologue," unpublished paper, 1980.

35. Colin Evans, "A Cultural View of the Discipline of Modern Languages," in *European Journal of Education*, XXV, #3 (1990), p. 281.

36. See *SSRC Annual Report, 1987-88*, pp. 13-24.

37. Tony Becher, "The Counter-Culture of Specialization," in *European Journal of Education*, XXV, #3, (1990), p. 339.

38. Charles J. Andersen, *International Studies for Undergraduates, 1987: Operations and Opinions* (Washington, DC: American Council on Education, 1988), p. ix.

39. Robert McCaughey, *International Studies and Academic Enterprise*, p. 245. See John Pincus, "Rand Meets the President's Commission: The Life-Cycle of a Non-Event," in *Annals of the American Academy of Political and Social Science*, 449 (May 1980), pp. 80-90.

40. John Brademas, "Internationalizing Higher Education," address delivered at the University of Michigan, May 8, 1992.

41. Richard J. Wood, President of Earlham College, "Toward Cultural Empathy: A Framework for Global Education," in *Educational Record*, 72, #4 (Fall, 1991), p. 10.

42. *Boston Globe*, January 12, 1992.

43. Lambert, *International Studies and the Undergraduate*, p. 112.

44. Craufurd D. Goodwin and Michael Nacht, *Missing the Boat: The Failure to Internationalize American Higher Education* (Cambridge: Cambridge University Press, 1991), p. 17. See also their instructive description of progress at the Colorado School of Mines, *ibid.*, pp. 105-09.

45. Lambert, *International Studies and the Undergraduate*, p. 150.

46. Quoted in Torsten Husen, *Education and the Global Concern* (Oxford: Pergamon, 1990), p. 147.

Foreign Student Flows and the Internationalization of Higher Education

* * * * * * * *

Richard D. Lambert

EXECUTIVE SUMMARY

Richard Lambert takes an in-depth look at foreign student flows to the United States and discusses factors that could affect the flow as well as the extent of foreign student contributions to the internationalization of American campuses.

The United States has the distinction of receiving the largest share of foreign students studying outside their own country. Over the past several years, there has been an overall increase in the number of foreign students who attend American universities, particularly at the graduate level. Lambert also points out that recent political and economic changes overseas have changed which countries send their students to the U.S. For instance, Asian students have replaced students from OPEC countries as a significant flow of foreign students to the U.S. Concerning recruiting trends of American universities, Lambert points out that American institutions in pursuit of foreign students typically seek out those who can pay their own way. Consequently, students from wealthy countries are more sought after than students from developing countries.

Factors that could affect the future flow of students are outlined. In addition to the prevailing economic and politi-

cal condition of foreign nations, which change over time, Lambert points out two other factors that will affect future flows: federal and institutional policies concerning the funding and enrollment of foreign students, and increasing competition for foreign students from other countries. Despite efforts by other countries to increase their share of foreign students, Lambert believes that American universities will continue to lead in this regard for many years to come. He cites several reasons for this belief, including the high investment in American institutions, the accessibility of American schools, and the distinction in this country between graduate and undergraduate education. Lambert also addresses another common concern: in an effort to obtain the best students, our research institutions have become too dependent on foreign graduate students whose skills in science and math are believed to be superior.

Lambert points out that the increased presence of foreign students at U.S. institutions does not necessarily help to internationalize American campuses. Those foreign students who come to the United States to study tend to be from the "wrong countries"—most foreign students are from Asia, while American students tend to learn European languages and want to study abroad in Europe. Morever, foreign students in this country are very rarely represented in international majors, choosing instead science, math, and engineering.

INTRODUCTION

The literature on international exchanges is voluminous. This essay emphasizes two aspects of such exchanges: the general impact of foreign student flows on the internationalization of campuses, and the scale and composition of future flows. It is difficult to imagine a world in which the hidden threads of student exchanges do not provide a durable fabric of amity that survives even the most rancorous of international disputes. And this is an area in which the United States is a recognized world leader. Moreover, even beyond the less tangible benefits of increased understanding, the United States has come to realize that the import of foreign students is a major asset on our international balance sheet. Charles Karelis, the director of the Fund for the Improvement of Post-Secondary Education, recently prepared for the

White House an assessment of the economic advantage to the United States of foreign students. He estimated that foreign students brought $3,351,000,000 to the United States.[1] The University of Iowa alone estimated that foreign students contributed $4 million annually to the local economy.[2]

AGGREGATE FLOWS

Overall Numbers of Foreign Students

In 1990-91 the Institute of International Education (IIE) census reported 407,529 foreign students registered in American colleges and universities. This represented an increase of 667% from the 53,107 students reported in 1960-61. The increase in numbers has been somewhat uneven across the intervening years, in some years slowing to an increase of barely 1%. Explosive growth of 172% between 1960 and 1970, and of 125% between 1970 and 1980 preceded growth of only 25% between 1980 and 1990. Current growth is at the rate of 5% annually, and the rate of overall increase is currently climbing again.

The proportion of foreign students in all higher education institutions has gone from 1.4% of students in 1960-61 to 2.9% in 1990-91. However, while the number of foreign students is increasing at a growing rate, and their proportion among all students is expanding, they still represent only a very small proportion of the total student body in all of American higher education. As will be seen, however, their representation in several important subsections of higher education is much more substantial.

Will this overall level of foreign student influx continue? Simple extrapolation will not provide the answer. Such extrapolation was attempted a decade ago in a national stocktaking review of foreign student flows.[3]

Prophesy concerning the scale of foreign student flows is a most hazardous enterprise. Foreign student flows operate in a complex, highly differentiated market in which most of the decisions are made overseas and on grounds not readily affected by institutional behavior in the United States. Hence, it is not surprising that past attempts at prognosis both as to numbers and sources of foreign students have been flawed by the need to extrapolate from the trends of the time. Who could predict the sea changes resulting from a revolution in Iran; OPEC oil revenues in the Middle East, Venezuela, and Nigeria; the economic surge of Japan and the other "tigers" of Asia; or the damage done to traditional Commonwealth student flows to Great Britain resulting from the Thatcher government's sudden introduction of discriminatory pricing for foreign students?

In the 1970s and 1980s, many people in higher education bet on the continuation of past country-specific sending patterns and believed that growing college and university commitment to campus-wide internationalization would lead to the recruitment of larger and larger complements of international students. The former prediction turned out to be incorrect: the complement of sending countries has undergone radical shifts. As will be noted below, events blessed the United States with development of new sources of foreign students as older sources declined. When OPEC countries faded as sources of foreign student recruitment, Asian countries made up the deficit.

The second prediction of continued expansion in the drive to internationalize campuses has been more accurate, although institutions and external funders are less and less willing to invest in such efforts. Moreover, the goal of cosmopolitanizing the campus has been reinforced by the need on many campuses for increases in the number of foreign students to help reach minimal enrollment goals. Hence, pressures to expand the number of foreign students has resulted in more and more aggressive overseas recruitment campaigns.[4]

In the 1960s and 1970s a number of institutions anticipated a general decline in enrollments, particularly at the undergraduate level, and developed active recruitment campaigns. An increasingly common practice is the dispatch of admissions officers on group recruitment tours arranged by private broker organizations. Interviews with broker organization representatives indicate that the trend is toward more and more prestigious institutions participating in their recruiting programs.

Some of these efforts, particularly in the heyday of the Iranian student flows, displayed in an extreme form the exuberance and unbridled entrepreneurship that some American educational enterprises are capable of. In the immediate past, much of this entrepreneurial energy has been centered in Japan, and much of it through negotiated institution-to-institution linkages. An IIE survey[5] counted 99 separate American initiatives seeking to establish partnership arrangements with Japanese universities and even cities. A similar "feeding frenzy" of American educational institutions is in progress in the former Soviet Union and Eastern Europe.

Some of these forms of recruitment have been quite imaginative. For instance, split-site arrangements where students rotate between overseas and American institutions are quite interesting examples of foreign student recruitment. The growing practice of establishing overseas clones of all or part of an American institution is a recruitment device for foreign students without making them leave home. Similarly, recent Japanese efforts at purchasing all or parts of colleges and universities in the United States, a practice similar to ones used in the Japanese export industry, make the definition of study in the United States less clear.

To police some of the least savory recruitment programs, a formal set of Guidelines for Ethical Recruitment Principles has been developed. While those standards are voluntary, they have been helpful in disciplining the recruitment process. The problems of ethics and quality control that such initiatives introduce are discussed at length in the IIE report on recent expe-rience with Japan. As both countries develop experience with the creation of constructive partnerships, the value of these guidelines as recruiting devices will become more evident.

Another trend within recruitment practices reflects a similar general trend in foreign student admissions. The financial press under which most institu-tions now operate has made them less willing to subsidize foreign students, particularly at the undergraduate level. Those managing foreign recruitment trips reported that more and more institutions are interested only in full-paid applicants, that is, those who can cover the full costs of their education out of their own resources. A typical recruitment trip now goes where wealthy fami-lies able to pay in full for their childrens' education can be found. Most recruitment trips are now to Asia, where the normal circuit includes Japan, Hong Kong, South Korea, Taiwan, and perhaps Thailand and Indonesia. The circuit does not include India, Pakistan, Sri Lanka, or any of the other devel-oping countries where the "fully-paid" market is likely to be weakest.

U.S. Position in Worldwide Student Movement

As Maureen Woodall, of the University of London Institute of Education, said in commenting on increases in the flow of foreign students to the United States: "This was a result of changing policies in the sending countries rather than any changes in the US policy toward foreign students."[6] Some of these changes, however, relate to other receiving countries not just sending coun-tries.

In making predictions about future trends in foreign student enrollments, it is well to remember that the United States is not the only major importer of students. There are many other traditional streams of international student migration, particularly movements of students from former colonies to uni-versities in former colonial countries. These universities often continue to serve as reference institutions for degrees awarded to students from former colonies. In addition to these remnants of colonial ties, other countries, such as France, the United Kingdom, Costa Rica, and India, have traditionally provided either general or specialized higher education for students from other countries in their region. Future student flows to the United States will depend a good deal on what happens within this network of traditional educational ties.

Currently, the United States receives only 35% of the 1,127,387 students who enroll in higher educational institutions outside their homelands, but it receives a larger share than any other country. Still, other countries do play a significant role in international exchanges: France receives 13.7% of all in-ternational students; Germany, 10%; the United Kingdom, 6.5%; and Canada, 3.1%. Moreover, in a substantial number of countries, foreign students com-prise a larger proportion of the student body in higher education. Ten countries have a higher representation of foreign students among their university-level students than does the United States, including almost all of the countries of Northern Europe.

Future American drawing power in the international student market will not only result from the slow drift in traditional patterns, but will be affected by the growth of intra-regional exchange agreements and by the success of very active foreign recruitment campaigns by a few countries, notably Australia, Germany, and Japan. All of these agreements and campaigns, however, are intra-regional rather than worldwide in scope.

Aside from the influence of developments in other countries and regions, American higher education has a major drawing power on its own. One reason for this is that the United States has developed an immensely attractive higher education system by investing in it more heavily than most other nations have in their systems.

But expenditures tell only part of the story. The elaboration of a higher education system is, in part, a reflection of the proportion of the public that enrolls in higher education. Only Canada approaches the United States in the proportion of total population enrolled in higher education.

American higher education has a significant advantage in the international foreign student marketplace because of comparatively high investments, the existence of many institutions of different types and levels, the maintenance of a high quality level in most parts of the system, and the tradition of relatively open access to many of these institutions. In few other countries are offerings quite so diverse and access quite so open as in the United States.

A unique advantage of higher education in the United States is the disarticulation of graduate school from baccalaureate education. In the United States students need not, in many institutions can not, attend the same institution for both undergraduate and graduate education. Moreover, the status of English as a world language should not be underestimated; it gives the U.S. an incomparable advantage over countries where instruction is in other languages.

There are, however, some downsides. A series of horror stories on the quality of life of foreign students has been given prominent space in newspapers around the world, particularly in Japan. The excesses of some recruiting efforts of American institutions and particularly of for-pay brokers both in the United States and Japan[7] have dampened enthusiasms. Some interviewees worried that the United States may be losing its unquestioned scientific, technological, and business superiority, and that the implicit value of American degrees to students once they return home will diminish. Little evidence was found that these factors have as yet caused any substantial diminution in flows.

INSTITUTIONAL DIFFERENCES

Very few American colleges and universities have no foreign students at all. There is some bunching of students from particular countries in particular parts of the United States—East Asians tend to go to the West Coast and the Northeast, Latin Americans to the South and Southwest, Scandanavian students to Wisconsin and Minnesota—and the preference of American students for "highly selective" institutions is repeated among foreign students. The dispersion of foreign students across our educational spectrum is remarkable. In 1990-91 the top 10 institutions, in terms of number of foreign students, enrolled only 8.8% of all the foreign students in the country, and the top 20 had 14.6%. And the share of the top institutions in the student flow is decreasing, not increasing. In 1984-85, 21.4% of the students were registered in the 10 leading institutions and 27.4% in the top 20. Some of the institutional dispersion of foreign students results from deliberate policy. For instance, the Malaysian goverment specifically set out to disperse its students more widely among American universities after establishing a single beachhead at Southern Illinois University in Carbondale. By and large, however, the widespread dispersion of foreign students is an interesting tribute to the operation of a highly differentiated market system in foreign student flows to the United States.

Campuses, of course, differ considerably in the number of foreign students they enroll. Table 1[8] lists the institutions with the greatest numbers of foreign students for a selected number of years going back to 1954-55. What is notable is the change over the years in the top ranking institutions.

TABLE 1				
Institutions with the Most Foreign Students, Selected Years, 1954-55 to 1990-91			
1954/55		**1959/60**	
Institution	Foreign Students	Institution	Foreign Students
Columbia Univ., Barnard, and Teachers Coll.	1,254	New York University	1,580
New York University	946	Columbia Univ., Barnard, and Teachers Coll.	1,146
University of Michigan, Ann Arbor	810	University of California, Berkeley	1,140
University of California, Berkeley	798	University of Michigan, Ann Arbor	1,109
Harvard University	721	University of Minnesota, Twin Cities	1,010
University of Illinois, Urbana and Chicago	594	University of Illinois, Urbana and Chicago	935
University of Southern California	569	University of Wisconsin-Madison	790
University of Minnesota, Minneapolis	530	Massachusetts Institute of Technology	770
Cornell University	488	Cornell University	751
University of Wisconsin-Madison	477	Harvard University	738

TABLE 1

INSTITUTIONS WITH THE MOST FOREIGN STUDENTS, SELECTED YEARS, 1954-55 TO 1990-91 (CONTINUED)

1964/65		1969/70	
Institution	**Foreign Students**	**Institution**	**Foreign Students**
New York University	2,986	New York University	4,182
University of California, Berkeley	2,588	Miami-Dade Community College	3,998
Columbia Univ., Barnard, and Teachers Coll.	2,353	University of California, Berkeley	2,904
University of Wisconsin-Madison	1,290	Columbia Univ., Barnard, and Teachers Coll.	2,796
Howard University	1,258	University of California, Los Angeles	2,197
University of Pennsylvania	1,232	University of Wisconsin-Madison	2,117
University of Michigan, Ann Arbor	1,181	University of Pennsylvania	1,699
University of Minnesota, Twin Cities	1,149	University of Washington	1,663
University of Illinois, Urbana	1,137	University of Illinois, Urbana	1,658
Harvard University	1,054	University of Minnesota, Twin Cities	1,624

1974/75		1979/80	
Institution	**Foreign Students**	**Institution**	**Foreign Students**
University of Southern California	2,111	University of Southern California	3,305
Howard University	2,066	Los Angeles City College	3,000
Columbia Univ., Barnard, and Teachers Coll.	1,905	Miami-Dade Community College	2,790
University of Wisconsin-Madison	1,869	Columbia Univ., Barnard, and Teachers Coll.	2,625
University of Minnesota, Twin Cities	1,679	Texas Southern University	2,585
University of California, Berkeley	1,571	University of Texas, Austin	2,354
University of Texas, Austin	1,533	University of Wisconsin-Madison	2,092
Miami-Dade Community College	1,485	University of Michigan, Ann Arbor	1,941
New York University	1,474	University of California, Los Angeles	1,907
Harvard University	1,414	University of Washington	1,880

1984/85		1990/91	
Institution	**Foreign Students**	**Institution**	**Foreign Students**
Miami-Dade Community College	4,316	Miami-Dade Community College[1]	5,757
University of Southern California	3,761	University of Southern California	3,886
University of Texas, Austin	3,286	University of Texas, Austin	3,867
University of Wisconsin-Madison	2,901	Boston University	3,633
Columbia Univ., Barnard, and Teachers Coll.	2,773	University of Wisconsin-Madison	3,565
Ohio State University, Main Campus	2,606	University of Pennsylvania	3,122
North Texas State University	2,570	Columbia University[2]	3,077
Southern Illinois University, Carbondale	2,565	Ohio State University, Main Campus	3,021
Boston University	2,462	University of Illinois at Urbana-Champaign	2,967
University of Houston-University Park	2,424	University of California, Los Angeles	2,921

[1]This figure includes 3,539 refugees. Next year, when Open Doors data do not include refugees, Miami-Dade's figures will be considerably lower.
[2]The figure for Columbia University no longer includes Barnard and Teachers Colleges.

SOURCE: *Open Doors 1990-91: Report on International Education Exchange.* (New York: Institute of International Education, 1991): page 68.

Generally, Ph.D. granting universities have the highest proportions of foreign students.

Will this pattern of distribution continue? In truth, no one knows. Since so much of the distribution is the result of individual student choices, systematic information on why foreign students choose one institution over another is needed before this question can be answered. However, there is very little information on what determines the institutional choices of foreign students. The wide and increasing dispersal of foreign students among our colleges and universities is one of the most remarkable features of foreign student flows.

However, it may be instructive to speculate, for a moment, on what changes a major deflation in foreign student flows might produce. The highly rated, high-name-recognition American institutions would probably continue to have more applicants than they can admit, and the trends discussed below toward graduate-level, high-technology education would probably increase the hold of the research unversities. However, the amazing web of existing transnational institutional ties, and the cloudy understanding most foreigners have of differences among American institutions, make it difficult to predict what the profile of foreign student distribution would be. A major increase in the number of foreign students would have an even more incalculable impact on the distribution of students among institutions.

It should be stressed, however, that for most institutions and most students, recruitment is not the issue. The applicant pool is already considerably larger than can be comfortably admitted. Moreover, institutions as a whole tend to control only part of their foreign student intake. While the admissions office normally controls the influx of undergraduate students, the recruitment and admission to graduate schools tends to be the property of the departments or schools, not the central administration. By and large, therefore, the determinants of foreign student flows are dispersed among the many students who choose to come, among the institutions that attract and accept them, and in the circumstances of the countries that send them.

FIELDS OF SPECIALIZATION

Increasingly, foreign students come to the United States not for arts and science disciplines but for training in business, engineering, the physical sciences, mathematics, and computer science. Together, these fields comprise more than half (56%) of all majors taken by foreign students. If one adds in those here to improve their English, it would include more than two-thirds of all students. With the decline of technical assistance training for the least developed countries, training in agriculture is now taken by only 2% of foreign students, and only 3% of these students come for training in education. Clearly, it is our training in science and technology that attracts foreign students.

Table 2 shows that the preference of foreign students for science and technology education is most clear at the graduate level. At the undergraduate level, business training draws the most students. At the graduate level, engineering is the principal draw. This trend is even more marked at the Ph.D. level. Data from the National Research Council show that this preference has been longstanding, and is increasing.

TABLE 2

FIELDS OF STUDY OF FOREIGN STUDENTS WITHIN ACADEMIC LEVEL, 1990-91

Field of Study	Academic Level		
	Undergraduate	Graduate	Other
Agriculture	0.9%	3.5%	0.1%
Business and Management	26.5	14.7	7.2
Education	1.9	4.6	1.1
Engineering	15.3	23.0	5.0
Fine and Applied Arts	5.5	3.8	3.0
Health Sciences	3.8	4.7	2.2
Humanities	2.2	6.2	1.1
Mathematics and Computer Science	9.1	10.4	2.9
Physical and Life Sciences	4.6	14.2	1.9
Social Sciences	6.5	9.5	1.7
Other	13.0	4.4	4.4
Intensive English Language	0.1	1.0	59.7
Undeclared	10.6	0.0	9.7
TOTAL	100.0	100.0	100.0

SOURCE: *Open Doors, 1990-91.* p. 72.

The shift to applied degrees is, of course, not found only among foreign students, but represents a trend among American students as well. Among foreign students, however, it highlights the dependence of continued foreign student flows on the continued reputation of American universities for excellence in these fields. Many observers worry that this reputation may be declining.

ACADEMIC LEVEL

Some institutions place limits on foreign undergraduate enrollments. For many years Michigan State University did not admit undergraduates at all. For state institutions, such as those in the California system, enrollment of undergraduate foreign students is controlled as part of the general limitations placed on out-of-state students. Undergraduate foreign students comprise an essentially marginal portion of the undergraduate student body on most campuses.

Some countries and world regions send mainly undergraduate students to study in the United States. Many of the Caribbean and Central American countries; Southeast Asian countries, except Singapore, Taiwan, and Hong Kong; the Sub-Saharan African countries; and Turkey in the Middle East, still send predominantly undergraduate students. Asians, in general, tend to be less well represented among undergraduate than graduate students, while the reverse is true of Latin Americans. If there is a general impression, it is that a country will send its students to the United States if it is itself lacking in prestigious higher education institutions. Where the in-country higher educational system has strong, prestigious institutions, and where the track from those institutions into high level employment is well established, neither students nor sponsors find American undergraduate liberal arts education attractive. Indeed, in many such countries, the liberal arts aspects of education are completed in secondary school, and at the university level the student is ready to specialize. Fitting an American liberal arts undergraduate education into an educational career is therefore difficult.

What is likely to happen in the future in undergraduate foreign student enrollments? In the long run, as countries develop their own baccalaureate educational systems and well-used tracks for funneling the graduates of that system into high-level occupations, the flow of students at the undergraduate level is likely to diminish. Some caution must be exercised in making such a prediction, however. It has been noted that Hong Kong has expanded immensely its indigenous higher education collegiate system, but the number of applications for admission to American institutions for first degrees has risen, not fallen.

> In 1965, there were only 1,000 first-degree places (for only 2% of Hong Kong's relevant age group) provided by two universities. . . . In 1990-91 there were five tertiary institutions funded by the University and Polytechnic Grants Committee offering a total of 7,250 first-year, first-degree places for about 8.5% of the relevant age group. By 1994 the government plans to double that number to 15,000, providing education for 18% of the relevant age group.[9]

In the period July through December 1991, the number of student visas issued by the United States Consulate increased by approximately 10% over the same period the previous year.

The hope for further expansion depends upon the emergence into the marketplace of other countries, like Malaysia, Indonesia, or Taiwan, that have meager indigenous educational resources and a sudden need for expanding their educated elite. Such countries, or wealthy families within them, must have the financial resources to send students to the United States, since 80% of foreign undergraduate students are supported by their own or their family's funds, and another 5% are supported by their country's government. And more and more institutions are tilting their admission process toward fully funded foreign students.

The surge in foreign graduate students is particularly evident in the production of Ph.Ds. The National Research Council reported that "Between 1960 and 1989 the number of doctorates awarded to non-U.S. citizens increased seven fold, from 1976 to 8195." This immense increase in the number of foreign Ph.Ds came at a time when the American clientele for Ph.D study was sharply declining. As Bowen and Rudenstine commented:

> The simply extraordinary increase in the number of foreign recipients of doctorates, particularly in the years since 1980, offset almost exactly the decline in the number of U.S. residents earning doctorates. Thus the apparent stability in the *overall* number of doctorates awarded annually since the early 1980's is highly misleading. The number of doctorates awarded to U.S. residents in all fields continued to decline until at least 1986.[10]

The NRC data show that this decline continued into 1989.[11]

The production of Ph.D.s gives only a partial reflection of graduate education. It omits professional and applied programs, and leaves out all of the students who do not go on to the Ph.D. Adding these students in makes it even more evident how important foreign students are to American graduate education today. The proportion of foreign students among all graduate students is striking. At the 19 Ph.D. granting universities in New York State, the median proportion of foreign graduate students was 12%, more than twice as high as the proportion of foreign undergraduate students. But it is in the elite research universities that the share of foreign enrollees among graduate students is most dramatic. While the 19 Ph.D. granting universities in New York State have a median ratio of 0.3 foreign graduate students for each foreign undergraduate student, and while California State University at Long Beach has an equivalent ratio of 0.3, the University of California system has a ratio of 2.5 foreign graduate students for each foreign undergraduate student, and the University of Pennsylvania has a ratio of 3 foreign graduate students for each foreign undergraduate. The Ivy League institutions taken as a whole show an even greater proportion of graduate students: 4.3 foreign graduate students for every foreign undergraduate student.

Questions about the future flow of foreign graduate students are uppermost in the minds of many university presidents, certainly many department chairs. However, reactions are ambivalent. On the one hand, the current situation places the institution as a cosmopolitan entrepot in which ideas and people move freely across national boundaries. On the other hand, it makes the graduate school establishment uncomfortably dependent upon a source of students that is largely beyond its control. The departments determine recruitment and admissions of graduate students. Moreover, graduate departments are the ultimate meritocracies. The dearth of qualified Americans and the relatively low preparation in math and science of those who do apply are matters of concern for graduate departments. To best serve the disciplines, particularly their future research streams, professors in graduate departments feel that they *must* admit only the very best students. In the sciences and engineering especially, the best students increasingly turn out to be foreign students.

The admission practices of universities in science and engineering have been studied in detail.[12] One feature of that system is worth noting here. Many scientific and engineering departments feel that their reputation and their future ability to draw top quality students depend on the quality of students they are training now. This feeling is particularly strong in advanced research training, where foreign students, who are not usually eligible for American government-sponsored training grants, are supported after their first or second year of training as research assistants and post-doctoral fellows on faculty research projects. The skill of the scientifically educated junior work force is an essential ingredient for successful research by faculty members. This, in turn, determines the prestige of both the individual faculty member and the department, and, completing the circle, is directly related to the quality of the students applying for admission. As the chair of one physical science department put it, "the best students read the international journals in deciding where to study. We are already in a difficult position because of the obsolescence of much of our equipment, to lower the quality of our graduate assistants would be a disaster." In the science and engineering departments, foreign students are important for more than numerical reasons. Both the training and research capacity of some of our best graduate departments would be in serious jeopardy if the flow of foreign students were to stop.

One major pressure against the continuation of the present flow of foreign graduate students is largely internal. Many people, both on and off the campus, view the dependency of American graduate departments on foreign students as tragic. Some critics are concerned not about foreign students, but about what the decline in the number of Americans among the high quality applicant pool portends for the future of the United States. Others are opposed to the foreign student flow itself. One argument is that foreign students represent a constant technology drain; due to their professional level when they are in the United States, they bring no technological expertise with them. Universities argue that the technology flows are long-term rather than only during a student's stay at the university. A second argument is that foreign students are usurping benefits that should flow to American students, particularly to the extent that they draw on public or institutional resources. This issue has become political in California. As that state goes through the budget-driven, radical downsizing of its higher education system, foreign student enrollments are likely to be early candidates for curtailment. Strong voices in Congress and state houses are also concerned with this issue. The response of universities is that they admit a larger proportion of the American applicants than foreign applicants. The Association of American Universities has just released the results of a major study of 39 institutions which shows clearly that this is the case. Sometimes the criticism of foreign student flows comes from American minority groups believing that resources going to foreign students should be spent to increase their own participation in higher education.

In addition to general arguments challenging the heavy representation of foreign graduate students, the Immigration and Naturalization Service has progressively tightened visa regulations and the conditions under which foreign students can seek employment. Every new regulation seems to hit foreign students hardest. Moreover, congressional pressures to tax foreign students has made many individuals and sending countries both nervous and irate.

All in all, it seems fair to say that the flow of foreign graduate students is likely to continue but there are strong pressures building that may curtail or reshape it.

THE ECONOMICS OF FOREIGN STUDENT FLOWS

Much of the extensive literature on the financial aspects of foreign student flows[13] stresses the importance of income from foreign student tuitions or the extra money that such students bring to the community. The general argument is made that since universities have relatively inelastic costs, foreign student tuitions should be considered as marginal income. Some authors even go so far as to argue that universities should charge lower fees to encourage foreign students to come. On the other hand, some state governments argue that foreign students should be required to pay at least the differential that out-of-state students pay, and possibly closer to the full actual cost of their education. It was, indeed, the institution of such a policy that disrupted foreign student flows to the United Kingdom. Australia's policy of plowing back into foreign student subsidies a portion of past student foreign fees represents an interesting intermediate position.

In view of the increasing importance of finances in campus policy making, it is surprising how few really hard-nosed cost-benefit analyses of foreign student flows on individual campuses are generally available.

Here, we wish to call attention only to a few selected elements relating to the economics of foreign students. First, most foreign students are paying their own way using their own or their family's money. The proportion of foreign students reporting no outside support has been remarkably constant at about 67% for the past five years. No one knows what the price elasticity is for foreign students. While there is evidence of a major shift due to price, government sponsorship for students is shifting to shorter term stays and, unless there is a special reason, away from "big ticket" universities. Interviews with exchange officials in sending nations indicate that in the newly rich countries of Asia, in Latin American monied families, and in some of the foreign government-sponsored programs, American higher education is still a financial bargain. University officials and students in European countries indicate that escalating costs are a problem, particularly in view of the subsidies that ERASMUS[14] and similar programs offer. Moreover, if the current trend in several European countries of turning student support from grants to loans continues, the high cost of American education may become a major factor. Furthermore, if American government plans go forward to tax foreign student income, it is difficult to estimate what effect this will have on student flows.

What does seem to have happened is that American institutions themselves are shifting their recruitment and admission policies to target only fully paying students, those who make no demands on university student support programs. This policy shift reinforces one of the trends noted below: the decline in the flow of students from the poor countries of Africa and Asia as well as from the non-elite classes in other developing countries. This trend is especially troublesome as American government support for technical assistance training programs is severely curtailed.

REGION AND COUNTRY OF ORIGIN

Students come to American campuses from almost every country of the world. While the number of foreign students coming to the United States has increased steadily over the past four decades, the countries from which the students come have changed radically. We have, in fact, been almost magically blessed. Just when one set of countries has peaked and faded, another set has come along to take its place (see Table 3). All regions of the world are sending an increasingly larger number of students to the United States. It is the share that each country and region provides that has changed over time.

Today, more than one-half (56.4%) of the foreign students come from Asian countries, primarily China, Japan, Taiwan, India, and South Korea, in that order. In 1954-55 Asia sent only 29.7% of the foreign students. Latin America and Canada, which sent 29.7% and 13.8%, respectively, in 1954-55, have declined to 11.8% and 4.6%, respectively. Many European Community countries report a rapid growth of students from other EC countries, in part due to the new European Economic Community connections through ERASMUS and COMETT.

Is it likely that this pattern will change and tilt away from the United States? First of all, expanding the flow of students will be difficult for many countries. Most Latin American countries are suffering economic problems, particularly with foreign exchange, that keep many potential migrant students at home. Several countries are actively trying to increase their intake of foreign students.[15] In Europe, France has always been a magnet, both for its former colonies, and for students from other European countries. France's priority for recruiting only in the upper end of high technology and student quality, and its current general societal concerns with managing immigrant flows from its former colonies, make quick expansion of the number of foreign students unlikely. In the 1980s, the total number of foreign students in France was fairly stable at around 120,000. More than half of those students were from Africa. Rising nativist sentiments in France are likely to curtail some of that intake. On the other hand, between 1985 and 1989 there was already a 39% increase in students from other European Community countries.

TABLE 3

FOREIGN STUDENTS BY WORLD REGION OF ORIGIN, 1954-55 TO 1990-91

Year	Africa		Asia		Europe		Latin America		Middle East		North America		Oceania		
	Foreign Students	% of Total	Foreign Students	% of Total	Foreign Students	% of Total	Foreign Students	% of Total	Foreign Students	% of Total	Foreign Students	% of Total	Foreign Students	% of Total	YEAR TOTAL[1]
1954/55	1,234	3.6	10,175	29.7	5,205	15.2	8,446	24.7	4,079	11.9	4,714	13.8	337	1.0	34,232
1955/56	1,231	3.4	11,625	31.9	5,504	15.1	8,474	23.2	4,239	11.6	5,042	13.8	353	0.9	36,494
1956/57	1,424	3.5	13,429	33.0	6,005	14.8	9,110	22.4	4,763	11.9	5,444	13.4	424	1.0	40,666
1957/58	1,515	3.5	14,786	34.1	6,837	15.8	9,212	21.2	5,115	11.8	5,354	12.3	495	1.1	43,391
1958/59	1,735	3.7	16,486	34.9	6,606	14.0	10,249	21.7	5,956	12.6	5,512	11.6	612	1.3	47,245
1959/60	1,959	4.0	17,808	36.7	6,392	13.2	9,428	19.4	6,477	13.	5,761	11.9	568	1.2	48,486
1960/61	2,831	5.3	19,988	37.6	6,702	12.6	9,626	18.1	7,096	13.4	6,128	11.6	658	1.2	53,107
1961/62	3,930	6.8	22,451	38.7	6,833	11.8	9,915	17.1	7,394	12.7	6,639	11.4	796	1.4	58,086
1962/63	4,996	7.7	24,728	38.2	7,923	12.2	11,021	17.0	7,887	12.2	7,089	11.0	948	1.5	64,705
1963/64	6,144	8.2	27,682	37.0	9,348	12.5	12,882	17.2	8,980	12.0	8,548	11.4	1,080	1.5	74,814
1964/65	6,855	8.4	30,640	37.4	10,108	12.3	13,657	16.6	9,977	12.1	9,338	11.4	1,265	1.5	82,045
1965/66	6,896	8.3	30,371	36.7	10,226	12.4	13,998	16.9	9,895	12.0	9,851	11.9	1,325	1.6	82,709
1966/67	7,170	7.2	34,999	34.9	14,207	14.2	18,182	18.1	11,401	11.4	12,230	12.2	1,635	1.6	100,262
1967/68	6,901	6.3	38,672	35.1	15,556	14.1	21,908	19.9	11,903	10.7	12,236	11.1	1,683	1.5	110,315
1968/69	6,979	5.8	44,212	36.4	16,453	13.6	23,438	19.3	12,338	10.2	12,948	10.7	1,869	1.5	121,362
1969/70	7,607	5.6	51,033	37.8	18,524	13.7	24,991	18.5	13,278	9.9	13,415	9.9	2,077	1.5	134,959
1970/71	8,734	6.0	56,459	39.0	18,306	12.7	29,820	20.2	14,840	10.3	12,732	8.8	1,995	1.4	144,708
1971/72	9,592	6.8	54,276	38.7	16,219	11.6	28,832	20.6	14,651	10.5	10,541	7.5	2,131	1.5	140,126
1972/73	11,465	7.8	56,486	38.7	16,296	11.2	28,383	19.4	16,278	11.1	9,805	6.7	2,107	1.4	146,097
1973/74	12,937	8.6	57,072	37.8	15,539	10.3	30,276	20.0	18,381	12.2	8,883	5.9	2,375	1.6	151,066
1974/75	18,400	11.9	58,460	37.8	13,740	8.9	26,270	17.0	23,910	15.5	8,630	5.6	2,650	1.7	154,580
1975/76	25,290	14.1	64,540	36.0	14,400	8.1	29,820	16.6	32,590	18.2	9,720	5.4	2,740	1.5	179,370
1976/77	25,860	12.7	70,020	34.5	16,700	8.2	37,240	18.4	38,490	18.9	11,420	5.6	3,150	1.6	203,070
1977/78	29,560	12.6	73,760	31.3	19,310	8.2	38,840	16.5	57,210	24.l3	12,920	5.5	3,810	1.6	235,510
1978/79	33,990	12.9	76,850	29.1	21,690	8.2	41,120	15.6	70,430	26.6	15,520	5.9	4,150	1.6	263,940
1979/80	36,180	12.6	81,730	28.6	22,570	7.9	42,280	14.8	83,700	29.2	15,570	5.4	4,140	1.4	286,340
1980/81	38,180	12.2	94,640	30.4	25,330	8.1	49,810	16.0	84,710	27.2	14,790	4.7	4,180	1.3	311,880
1981/82	41,660	12.8	106,160	32.5	28,990	8.9	55,360	17.0	74,390	22.8	15,460	4.7	4,000	1.2	326,300

TABLE 3

Foreign Students by World Region of Origin, 1954-55 to 1990-91 (continued)

Year	Africa		Asia		Europe		Latin America		Middle East		North America		Oceania		
	Foreign Students	% of Total	Foreign Students	% of Total	Foreign Students	% of Total	Foreign Students	% of Total	Foreign Students	% of Total	Foreign Students	% of Total	Foreign Students	% of Total	YEAR TOTAL[1]
1982/83	42,690	12.7	119,650	35.5	31,570	9.4	56,810	16.9	67,280	19.9	14,570	4.3	4,040	1.2	336,990
1983/84	41,690	12.3	132,270	39.0	31,860	9.4	52,350	15.5	60,660	17.9	15,670	4.6	4,090	1.2	338,890
1984/85	39,520	11.6	143,680	42.0	33,350	9.7	48,560	14.2	56,580	16.5	15,960	4.7	4,190	1.2	342,110
1985/86	39,190	9.9	156,830	45.6	34,310	10.0	45,480	13.2	52,720	15.3	16,030	4.7	4,030	1.2	343,780
1986/87	31,580	9.1	170,700	48.8	36,140	10.3	43,480	12.4	47,000	13.4	16,300	4.7	4,230	1.2	349,610
1987/88	28,450	8.0	180,540	50.7	38,820	10.9	44,550	12.5	43,630	12.2	16,360	4.6	3,620	1.0	356,190
1988/89	26,430	7.2	191,430	52.2	42,770	11.7	45,030	12.3	40,200	11.0	16,730	4.6	3,610	1.0	366,350
1989/90	24,570	6.4	208,110	53.8	46,040	11.9	48,090	12.4	37,330	9.7	18,590	4.8	4,010	1.0	386,850
1990/91	23,800	5.9	229,830	56.4	49,640	12.2	47,580	11.8	33,420	8.1	18,950	4.6	4,230	1.0	407,530

[1]Includes students classified as stateless or of unknown origin.

Source: *Open Doors*, 1990-91, p. 16.

Germany is currently making a special effort to recruit more foreign students, particularly those in high technology and scientific fields. Germany traditionally draws its students from Greece, Austria, Turkey, the United States, Iran, and, to a limited extent, South Korea. Germany also draws heavily from Indonesia as a result of an earlier investment in financial and educational aid to that country. However, Germany is also insisting that its students master English to make them more mobile in the world community. Eastern Europe, where in many places German is the lingua franca, will no doubt loom large in future recruitment. Moreover, Germany is investing heavily in spreading German language competency both abroad and for incoming students wishing to study at German universities.

For years the United Kingdom has been a formidable magnet, particularly for drawing in students from the Commonwealth countries. Intra-Commonwealth exchanges dropped sharply in the 1970s and 1980s. The government became alarmed by the cost of supporting an increasing influx of foreign students, including American students, and introduced a double pricing system in which foreign students were required to pay "full costs." This policy immensely depressed foreign student flows. In fact, the United States was an unintended beneficiary of this policy in the case of Malaysia, which experienced a major upswing in study abroad that sent about 3,000 students to 541 different American colleges and universities.[16] The outcry in the Commonwealth countries against this double pricing policy was so strong that the government was forced to reinstate a selective fellowship program for some of the least developed of the Commonwealth countries. A 1987 statement by Malcolm Anderson of the University of Edinburgh described the reaction among advocates of international exchanges to the government's pricing policy:

In Britain, overseas student policy is at best equivocal, resulting in the small investment of resources and in the absence of clear political direction. Although recent developments may give some grounds for cautious optimism, a coherent student strategy, based on a recognition of the importance of cultural diplomacy, remains a long way off.[17]

Since that time, the short-lived deficit has been reversed, perhaps providing evidence on the price elasticity of foreign student flows. The various European Community exchange programs are the unknown factor in determining the future direction of foreign flows among European countries. If ERASMUS is fully implemented, 10% of the university student body in each European country will spend at least a part of their educational time in another European country. There are also supplemental programs, such as COMETT, which focuses on business, professional, and high technology flows, and TEMPUS, which focuses on flows from Eastern Europe. The effect of these programs on the flow of foreign students is still uncertain. The administrators of these programs insist that the programs should increase, rather than diminish, the number of students coming to the United States. They point out that these programs may encourage overseas studies by students who are not accustomed to venturing out, and that universities will move away from the bilateral exchange agreement formats that these programs entail and be encouraged to legitimize study abroad more generally. Already some 20% of ERASMUS students travel on their own. In addition, the Fund for the Improvement of Post-Secondary Education has signed an agreement for a pilot project on the ERASMUS model.

Eastern Europe and the former Soviet Union are likely to be major new sources for recruiting foreign students. However, since neither region has much money, bringing these students to the United States will require considerable investment of college or university resouces or major new support programs by the federal government.

The two countries that threaten to compete with the United States for Asian students are Australia, which is actively recruiting in Southeast Asia, and Japan, which is recruiting in Asia more generally. In both countries, expansion of the number of foreign students has been given explicit sanction by government. Australia has initiated a closely watched strategy whereby all tuition subsidies for foreign students will be reallocated to newly arrived overseas students through an Equity and Merit Scholarship program. However, Australia has a limited capacity to absorb large numbers of foreign students into its universities and, indeed, there are some indications of serious problems within that program. Japan's plans for attracting more foreign, particularly Asian, students is heavily funded by a major government foundation, and is ambitious. In 1991 there were 45,000 foreign students in Japan; by the end of the decade, the Japanese government has committed itself to hosting

100,000 foreign students. There are, however, a number of restraints on the drawing power of Japan for foreign students, including limitations on available housing, the proficiency in Japanese among potential foreign students, and the inhospitality of Japanese institutions to foreign student needs.

Countries and world regions differ considerably in their use of American higher education. By way of contrast, consider several of the principal sending countries and areas. The most numerous group of foreign students enrolled in American universities and colleges are Chinese. Conversely, the large majority (70.8%) of Chinese students who study abroad go to the United States. Australia is making a concerted effort to recruit Chinese students as part of its Asian initiative and currently 14.9% of the Chinese studying abroad go to that country. However, the European countries are so absorbed in expanding their exchanges among the countries of Europe that they are unlikely to recruit many Chinese, or for that matter, many Asians other than those in Commonwealth countries.

Chinese students comprise 9.7% of all foreign students in the United States, some 39,600 students in all in 1990-91. However, because of their clustering by institution, by majors, and by section of the country, they appear to be more numerous. In spite of unsettled political events in China, 6,200 more students reached the United States last year and many members of previous student cohorts have been given refugee status. The continued flow of Chinese students in the face of intense government efforts to restrain them is remarkable. They are exceedingly well-organized and have considerable skill in mastering the intricacies of INS visa and work requirements. The Chinese come to the United States almost exclusively for graduate study (82%). About one-fourth of the Chinese undergraduates major in business, but the rest spread out across other disciplines. Chinese graduate students tend to concentrate heavily on the physical sciences (fully 33% at the graduate level); engineering (21%), especially electrical engineering; and math and computer science (14%). Together these disciplines absorb about two-thirds of Chinese graduate students. In many universities, these students sustain physical science and engineering departments, as the number and quality of American applicants drop off. The loss of Chinese students would be a major blow to American higher education.

Japanese students comprise the second largest and the fastest growing foreign student group. Their pattern of study is somewhat different from the Chinese and other foreign students. Business and management continue to be the most popular majors of Japanese students, but the number of students interested in American business training is dropping. Their participation in engineering is also declining. Many Japanese do not think we have much more to impart in these fields. In many ways, the Japanese study abroad pattern is like our own. They often come for language training and some exposure to the country rather than academic content; they tend to cluster in a relatively few institutions, particularly those that have formal links with a Japanese university; they tend to be totally self-supporting and they tend to enclave on campus for mutual support. The change in the exchange rate between the yen and the dollar has made it relatively inexpensive for the Japanese to study in the United States. The future of Japanese-American student exchanges is of great interest to the United States. Indeed, special efforts are being made to link the two-way student flows[18] between the two countries.

Africans are in real jeopardy of disappearing from the foreign student scene; students from South Africa, where recruiting efforts are currently underway, are the possible exception. The number of African students enrolled in the United States has declined in each of the past 10 years. Sending students to the United States is a major expense, and, since the United States Agency for International Development (AID) has radically cut its training grants, the numbers of African students have shrunk immensely. They are likely to decline even more sharply in the future. It is a pity that some of the links built with African universities over the past several decades are likely to dry up, both because of what is happening in those institutions themselves and because of the search for fully supported students by American universities.

Experts on Latin America believe that exchanges will remain at about the same level. Latin American students currently comprise about one-eighth of all foreign students. The flow of Latin American students is traditionally sustained by well-to-do families sending their children to America to acquire a degree, and this is likely to continue. The one country where expansion might be substantial is Mexico. In conjunction with the passage by Congress of the North American Free Trade Agreement (NAFTA) linking the United States with Mexico and Canada, there is currently discussion of ways to make it easier for students from the United States and Mexico to enroll in each others' institutions. In addition, if the loan swap arrangements such as those pioneered at Harvard really develop, Latin America could once again be a major recruiting ground.

The traditional sender countries in the Middle East are Iran and Saudi Arabia. Student migration from both countries has declined precipitously since a peak at the height of OPEC's influence, and will probably continue to decline. A substantial flow of Egyptian students continues to come under Egyptian government sponsorship. Indeed, Fulbright sends only post-doctoral students to the United States from that country. Tuition paying students are either here on their own funds or on those of their government. Increasingly, these students are more mature, come for shorter periods of time, and go to moderately priced universities. Israel, with only 3,000 students, is hardly a blip on the screen, and, given the speed and level of development of the Israeli higher education system, is unlikely to be a major source of recruitment.

FOREIGN STUDENTS AND INTERNATIONALIZATION OF THE CAMPUS

In one sense, foreign students on a campus are de facto a force for internationalization. This is particularly true of research universities that see as part of their function the education of the scientific and technical elites of the world. If one shifts attention, however, to other aspects of the internationalization of the campus, particularly those that serve to cosmopolitanize the education of American students—foreign language study, study abroad, internationally oriented courses and majors—linkages with foreign student flows become very weak. Foreign students have almost no connection with the most common international courses that most American students take: foreign language courses. While some may serve as native speaker informants in area studies programs, by and large foreign students speak the "wrong" languages: most of them come from Asian countries while most American students are studying Spanish, French, or German. Nor are they well represented as students in international courses and majors. They tend to concentrate in the technical and natural science fields where internationalization is least relevant; in large universities, even casual contacts with most American students are minimal. Nor is there any substantial link between foreign students and the flow of American students going abroad to study. Again, they come from the wrong countries. Most study abroad programs take American students to England, France, or Germany, while most foreign students come from Asia, or perhaps Latin America. Moreover, the numbers of American students studying abroad and of foreign students coming to the United States are quite uneven. Open Doors: 1990-91[19] reported only 70,727 American college or university students (less than 0.1%) were enrolled in formal study programs abroad, while 407,529 foreign students (2.9% of all students) were registered in American institutions of higher education. And finally, most international studies programs are aimed at undergraduates while the proportion of foreign undergraduate students on most campuses is relatively small.

If one of the abiding issues in internationalizing a campus is how to make its components more symbiotic and mutually reinforcing, only modest progress has been made in this direction.

SUMMARY AND CONCLUSIONS

Predicting the future of foreign student flows to the United States requires a careful analysis of a number of different aspects of current aggregate trends.

The total number of foreign students has been increasing, but with some substantial changes over time in the rate of increase. Whether it will continue to grow depends on future developments in various separate elements of the flow. Foreign students are spread widely throughout the American higher education system. Some narrowing of the spread is contemplated. In most institutions foreign students comprise less than 10% of all students, but in the Ivies and other research universities they make up a higher percentage of the student body. In part, this is due to a major shift among foreign students toward graduate rather than undergraduate education, and toward science, engineering, and business disciplines as the subjects they seek to study. The most striking feature of this shift is the heavy dependence of many research-oriented departments in engineering, mathematics, and science on foreign students, particularly those from China and other Asian countries, for both enrollments and for student assistants in faculty research projects. The pattern of support for foreign students in the sciences and engineering, which begins with university grants and fellowships at the outset followed by funding for students as research assistants or post-doctoral fellows on faculty research projects, is a fragile system that may be difficult to sustain in the long run.

Changes in the countries and regions sending foreign students to the United States have been substantial, but the total flow has continued to grow. One country or set of countries seems to emerge to send large numbers of students to the United States as other countries or regions have subsided. The different characteristics of student flows from various regions and countries have been discussed, together with some developments that may affect future flows from each region.

Finally, foreign student flows intrinsically result in some internationalization of the campus, but there are structural disjunctions between the foreign student presence on the campus and other aspects of international studies—language study, study abroad, courses and concentrations dealing with other countries—that are concerned with the cosmopolitanization of American students.

At the close we return to the opening comment: the flow of foreign students is of immense value to our society in general and to the individual institutions they attend. It is to be hoped that other countries will continue to send us some of their most gifted students and that current problems and pressures within the United States will not diminish our ability to provide them with the best education that our colleges and universities have to offer.

NOTES

1. Letter from Charles Karelis to Steve Dansansky, February 4, 1992.
2. This statistic was taken from a chart prepared by Frederick Lockyear of International Advisory Services for a presentation at the NAFSA-AIE Conference in Chicago, May 23, 1992.
3. Committee on Foreign Students and Institutional Policy, *Foreign Students and Institutional Policy* (Washington, DC: American Council on Education, 1982), p. 56.
4. For an excellent review of the history of recruitment efforts, see Cassandra Pyle, "Changes in the Landscape: Forces Shaping Recruitment in the 1990's" (Boston: NAFSA Field Service Seminar, May 27, 1991).
5. Gail S. Chambers and William K. Cummings, *Profiting from Education* (New York: Institute of International Education, 1990).
6. Maureen Woodall, "Government Policy Toward Overseas Students: An International Perspective" in Gareth Williams, Martin Kenyon, Lynn Williams, eds., *Readings in Overseas Student Policy* (London: Overseas Students Trust, 1987), p. 29.
7. For a detailed examination of the problems and promises in this situation, see Chambers and Cummings, *Profiting from Education*.
8. Reprinted from *Open Doors, 1990-91*, p. 68.
9. Marsha Lee, IIE advisor in Hong Kong.
10. William G. Bowen and Neil L. Rudenstine, *In Pursuit of the PHD* (Princeton, NJ: Princeton University Press, 1992), p. 28.
11. Delores H. Thurgood and Joanne M. Weinman, *Summary Report 1989: Doctorate Recipients from United States Universities*. National Research Council, Office of Science and Engineering Personnel (Washington, DC: National Academy Press, 1990), p. 56.
12. For a detailed analysis of admission and enrollment processes in biochemistry, economics, mathematics, and mechanical engineering, see R.H. Harriott, "Competitive Access to Contemporary American Doctoral Education: A Comparative Analysis of U.S. and non-U.S. Citizens in Four Science and Engineering Fields." AAU-AGS Project for Research on Doctoral Education. Unpublished manuscript, University of Rochester, 1991. For a report on foreign student attitudes toward engineering education, see Elinor G. Barber, Robert P. Morgan, and William P. Darby, *Choosing Futures: U.S. and Foreign Student Views of Graduate Engineering Education* (New York: Institute of International Education, 1990).
13. See, for instance, Committee on Foreign Students and Institutional Policy, *Foreign Students and Institutional Policy*, Chapter 4; Donald G. Ehrensberg, "The Flow of New Doctorates" *Journal of Economic Literature* 30 (June 1992), pp. 830-75; John Fielden and Hew Dalrymple, "Flexibility in Setting Fees" in Williams, Kenyon, and Williams, *Readings in Overseas Student Policy*, pp. 115-20; C.D. Throsby, "The Financial Impact of Foreign Student Enrollments" *Higher Education* 21 (April 1991), pp. 351-58.
14. For information on actual operation of ERASMUS programs, see Ulrich Teichler, "Experiences of Erasmus Students: Select Findings of the 1988-89 Survey,"

ERASMUS Monographs 13, Werkstattberichte 32 (Kassel, Germany: Gesamthochschule, Kassel Universität, 1991).

15. For a review of the exchange policies of Great Britain, France, Germany, Japan, Australia, and Canada, see Alice Chandler, *Obligation or Opportunity: Foreign Student Policy in Six Major Receiving Countries* (New York: Institute of International Education, 1989).

16. *Report on Malaysian Students Entering U.S. Educational Institutions—1987* (Kuala Lumpur: Malaysian-American Commission on Educational Exchange, 1987), p. 3.

17. Malcolm Anderson, "Overseas Students and British Foreign Policy" in Williams, Kenyon, and Williams, *Readings in Overseas Student Policy*, p. 33.

18. Norman J. Peterson and John Skillman, "Shifting the Balance: Increasing U.S. Undergraduates in Japan," A report to Culcon, 1992.

19. *Open Doors 1990-91: Report on International Educational Exchanges* (New York: Institute of International Education, 1991), pp. 84 and 13, respectively.

Trends in Higher Education and Its Finance in Western Europe

* * * * * * * *

Gareth Williams

EXECUTIVE SUMMARY

Gareth Williams provides a glimpse of recent trends in the higher education systems of 12 European Community countries. Unlike American institutions, which have much in common, each of these 12 countries has its own distinct higher education system. Williams describes the two broad approaches to how higher education is provided in the European Community. State provision has been the dominant model in France and is followed closely by most other European countries, while Great Britain, until recently, has relied almost exclusively on private initiatives. In many European countries, a substantial non-university sector accounts for more than half of total enrollments; the focus in these types of institutions is more on professional preparation and less on research. Williams also points out the vast differences among the countries in the total expenditures in the form of grants to students, ranging from 25% in Great Britain to 10% in France. In general, each of the Western European governments plays a prominent role in the provision of higher education. The exceptions are Italy and Spain, where higher education has "retained its traditional academic characteristics" and consists of universities only; however, the drop-out rates in these countries are consider-

ably higher than in the other countries. Germany has the most bureaucratically controlled institutions.

Williams discusses the age of students and course structures, degree of institutional autonomy, and mechanisms of finance. He also cites a number of initiatives now underway that address how higher education is financed in the European Community. The most important of these is the development of formulas to determine the funding allocation to institutions. One such formula allocates funds based on the number of students who actually complete the courses. Several countries are also considering charging the students fees to help pay for higher education. Many worry that these and other changes might increase the financial and academic disparities among universities or that an excessive amount of staff time will need to be devoted to preparing proposals and accounting for how funds are used.

Since the 1980s, Great Britain has experienced a number of changes in the way its higher education is funded, changing from a loosely monitored formula by a single government agency to a closely specified formula by a wider variety of public and private funding bodies. Williams describes how a 10% decline in regular public expenditures has, curiously, resulted in some positive outcomes: the number of graduates rose by 10% and the number of higher degrees rose by 60%. Income generation from the sale of teaching and research services has gone up, and rewards have been offered to staff members who generate supplemental income. Williams observed that many see this and other changes as "a departure from the traditional collegiality of the British university."

Two initiatives in the European community are of note. First is what Williams refers to as the "harmonization of professional qualifications." Because there are such disparities in the curriculums in most European institutions, not to mention the number of years it takes to obtain degrees in certain fields, National Academic Recognition Centers have been established that provide employers and prospective students with information on the value and recognition of educational credentials in other countries. Second, student and staff mobility among European higher education institutions has been promoted through the European Community Action Scheme for Mobility of University Students

(ERASMUS) and the Trans-European Mobility Scheme for University Students (TEMPUS).

INTRODUCTION

The higher education systems of European countries are as different from each other as any one of them is from that of the United States. Each of the 12 countries of the European Community has a distinct higher education system. In the U.S., the 51 different state systems have much in common: degree structures are more or less uniform across the whole country and recognized conventions permit common reporting of student and staff numbers and the main income and expenditure magnitudes. None of this exists in Europe at present. The European Community is moving towards the development of formally recognized qualification equivalences, but there is a long way to go before even superficial similarity is achieved. Developing such equivalences would encourage student mobility between different countries and contribute to the free European labor market that is due to come into operation on January 1, 1993. Problems are caused by the wide variety of different national arrangements for institutional funding and student financial support, and several individual cases have come before the European Courts, but the current concern with national sovereignty makes it unlikely that any significant harmonization of national policies for higher education will occur in the foreseeable future.

This essay begins with a brief outline of, and recent trends in, the higher education systems of the countries of the European Community, both their academic structures and their main funding mechanisms. A discussion of recent developments in funding of institutions and students follows. A special section covers developments in Great Britain since 1988; changes in that country have been particularly radical, but are also illustrative of similar, if less pronounced, trends elsewhere in Western Europe. A short section discusses European Community initiatives on higher education, and the essay concludes with an attempt to draw some conclusions and some speculations about possible future developments.

EUROPEAN HIGHER EDUCATION SYSTEMS

There have been two broad approaches to the provision of higher education in Europe. One is state provision of a public service, often linked in part to the preparation of future servants of the state; the other is private initiative based largely on altruism but also on entrepreneurial activity. The former has traditionally been the dominant model in France, while the latter has always been the main characteristic of higher education in Great Britain, where government did not become involved at all until 1919, and not seriously until after the Second World War. In some respects, the 1988 Education Reform Act underlined the traditional legal and financial autonomy of universities by transforming all significant higher education institutions into independent statutory corporations.

Most Western European countries have been closer to the French model than the British, but there has been considerable convergence in recent decades. In Great Britain, government has intervened more and more directly in higher education through its control of finance and its insistence on academic accountability in the use of public funds. In many other Western European countries, the inherent inefficiencies of direct administrative control of universities is leading to more devolution of management responsibilities to the universities themselves. However, in several countries, including France and Germany, the academic staff of universities remain public sector employees paid directly by the state.

In Great Britain the establishment in 1919 of the University Grants Committee as a "buffer" between universities and government enabled the national government to provide a "deficiency grant" to universities without becoming directly involved in any aspect of their operation. The lack of viability of this arrangement in a vastly expanded higher education system that had come to depend almost entirely on public funds helps to explain the convulsions that British universities have experienced over the past decade.

In some European countries, the Church still controls a few universities. For the most part, however, the trend until the early 1980s was for private and other independent universities to be absorbed, at least de facto into the state sector as they became more and more dependent on public funds.

In all major European countries except Spain and Italy, and, since 1991 Great Britain, there is a substantial non-university sector; much of the expansion in enrollments since the 1970s has been in this sector. In several countries, non-university higher education now accounts for more than half of total enrollments.[1] For the most part these institutions focus more on professional preparation and less on research than the universities and are funded less generously, but the pattern is by no means uniform.

In a major comparative study in 1992 for the European Community, Frans Kaiser and his colleagues[2] draw attention to the arbitrary and inconsistent definitions of what constitutes a university in European countries and, in particular, "the rather vague lines of demarcation between university and non-university education in so called multi-purpose and comprehensive systems of higher education" These authors define a university as being "of academic standard and closely linked with scientific research." They claim that universities proper are distinguished by "the presence of research activities. . . and the general requirement that faculty members hold higher qualifications." This, they claim, explains the "relatively higher level of (per student) expenditure" in the university sector. However, in its 1992 Higher and Further Education Act, the British government explicitly rejected this view of "the university." Most of the institutions that were previously called polytechnics, together with a significant number of other colleges, have been redesignated as universities with no explicit changes in their missions. It is generally accepted that research will play only a minor role in many institutions now designated as universities.[3]

The definition of *expenditure* on higher education is even more varied. Kaiser et al. distinguish two main issues: "firstly what *types* of expenditures are included, and secondly *whose* expenditures are included." Their concern is mainly to draw attention to the distinction between expenditure on higher education *institutions* and expenditure on *student* living costs, but the problem is more complicated than that. For example, in France and Germany, the salaries of established academic staff are paid directly by government so university expenditure often includes only nonacademic staff salaries, whereas in Great Britain it is usual to include all expenditure by autonomous universities as higher education. Capital expenditure in general is extraordinarily difficult to compare and is usually left out of international comparisons.

The treatment of research also varies. In some countries, such as Germany and Great Britain before the mid-1980s, a considerable but unspecified proportion of the expenditure on universities is deemed to be for research, whereas in France most research is funded out of a separate budget and is commonly not included in figures of higher education expenditure.

The differing roles of public and private expenditure in different countries provide another difficulty. This is most obvious in the case of financial support to students. In Great Britain, well over a quarter of total expenditure on higher education is in the form of maintenance grants to students, whereas in France the corresponding figure is 10%. Figures of expenditure on higher education in France, therefore, ignore student living costs, which are often included with higher education expenditure in Great Britain since they are subsidized to a very considerable extent out of public funds.

The legal status of universities varies from independent but closely regulated corporations in the United Kingdom to what are in effect government departments in Germany. In a few countries, such as Spain, Portugal, and Belgium, the Church runs a number of universities but their legal and financial status is little different from those run directly by public authorities. There has been a little development of private universities during the past 10 years, such as the University of Buckingham in England, but these institutions operate on a very small scale at the margins of public higher education institutions.

In general, Western European governments play a prominent part in the provision of higher education and there tends to be relatively little variety of provision within countries. At the extreme are Italy and Spain where "higher education is to be considered as largely synonymous with university education."[4]

In Italy "university education has retained its traditional academic characteristics and predominantly offer *corsi di laurea* (degree courses)."[5] In 1988, 1.22 million students were enrolled in 44 public and 11 private universities. Fees are low in the public universities but there is virtually no financial support for students' living costs either as grant or loan. Private universities depend to a considerable extent on fees, but most are relatively inexpensive. It is not an efficient system. During recent years the number of secondary school students who pass the matriculation examination (*maturita*), which qualifies them for entry to a university, has been about 40% of the relevant age group and about 65% of these enter higher education. Of these, about 30% (or 8% of the age group) ultimately obtain the *laurea* (bachelor's degree), often taking considerably longer than the prescribed four years to do so. There is to all intents and purposes no intermediate level of qualification, so most of the remaining 70% of university entrants leave without a recognizable qualification.

In Spain, as in Italy, the higher education system consists of universities only and is characterized by high student dropout. Of 35 universities, 31 are public and 4 belong to the Roman Catholic Church and operate under a special treaty with the Vatican. "A striking characteristic of the Spanish university sector is the limited number of degrees (and therefore of programs) offered, especially when it is taken into account that there is no non-university sector."[6] There has been no major reform of the structure of courses or programs offered since engineering was introduced in the 1920s. An ambitious University Reform Law in 1983 increased the autonomy of universities and strengthened their research base but did not change the structure of degree programs. In Spain, as in Italy, fewer than half the entrants to first degree courses (*diplomado*) leave with a qualification and the remainder receive no formal recognition of their performance.

Institutional finance in Spain differs in one important respect from Italy: student fees make a significant contribution to institutional income. They averaged about $500 at the end of the 1980s in public universities and accounted for about 20% of the income of universities. Apart from this, Spain belongs to the group of countries in which almost the whole of the income of universities comes in the form of an institutional subsidy from public funds.

Financial support for students is modest and concentrated on the very poorest. In 1986/87 it averaged $115 per student.

These two countries have, since 1992, been joined by Great Britain where over 80% of students are now in institutions designated as universities. Most other European countries have two or more distinct sectors of higher education with perceptibly different "missions."

France has three distinct major categories of higher education institutions. The highest status institutions are not the universities but the "Grandes Ecoles," highly specialized teaching institutions originally established long before the Revolution, but much strengthened by Napoleon to prepare an elite corps of professionals for the service of the state. Unlike the rest of French higher education, these great schools have the right to apply very strict and competitive entrance criteria based on examination performance and their final examinations are also very competitive, with graduates able to choose their preferred field of government employment in the order of their marks on the final examinations. In some respects, the Grandes Ecoles have the same privileged position in relation to the rest of the higher education system as the great National Universities of Japan. Most of the top positions in both the public and private sectors of the French economy are filled by alumni of the Grandes Ecoles.

Below the universities, but closely linked to them, are a number of "short cycle" institutions, offering highly specialized courses of two years or shorter. These institutions consist mainly of the Instituts Universitaires de Technologie (IUTs), which are linked to universities but academically and administratively distinguished from them. They were created in the early 1970s as a new stream within the first (short) cycle, with the aim of training technicians in a wide variety of fields. They were established at the same time as the British polytechnics, but, unlike the polytechnics, have had a clear definition of role; like the Grandes Ecoles, but unlike the British polytechnics (before they were transformed into universities), they have a selective entry, which has done much to ensure their distinct academic mission.

Student drop out is low from the selective Grandes Ecoles and IUTs but high in the universities where about 50% of students leave without a qualification. One reason for the establishment of the two-year first cycle was to enable students who were unlikely to complete a full four-year course to obtain a qualification (the Diplome d'Etudes Universitaires Generales—DEUG) that has some value in the labor market.

France is similar to Italy in its heavy reliance on government funding, the virtual absence of fees in public universities, and the relatively low levels of financial support to students. Average direct financial support per student in 1988 was about $200; this was supplemented by about $50 worth of "indirect aid" in the form of subsidized accommodation, meals, etc. About 90% of the income of institutions comes directly from central government funds.

Another distinct feature of French higher education, as compared with most other European countries, is the sharp distinction between funding of research and teaching. The Grandes Ecoles and universities are funded primarily as teaching institutions. Research is funded by the Centre National de la Recherche Scientifique (CNRS) but many of its research establishments are located on or close to university campuses and there is a good deal of cross-fertilization in the form of academic staff having appointments in both. There is, however, little financial cross-subsidization and French statistics of expenditure of higher education institutions often ignore much research expenditure. The sharpening of the separation between teaching and research is another marked trend in British higher education, but it remains normal to include research as part of the reported income and expenditure of universities.

In this respect, France is almost at the opposite extreme from Germany. Funding of higher education institutions in Germany is probably the most bureaucratically controlled in Europe. Nearly all the expenditure on academic staff salaries is paid directly to the individuals by the appropriate Land Ministry of Education. Remaining income is *not* earmarked for teaching or research but the expenditure of universities *is* rigidly controlled by input categories such as salaries, equipment, teaching materials, travel expenses, and so on. Universities are required to adhere to these budget headings closely in spending their budgets and they are not allowed to carry forward any surpluses from one year to the next.

German higher education also has a number of other distinct features. It is a binary system with a university and a non-university sector, but it is unique in Europe in that it is a federal system with higher education institutions firmly under the control of the governments of the 11 *länder* or states. There is some federal legislation; for example, the federal "Framework Law" sets out general principles, of which the most important is the unconstitutionality of charging student fees. The *Bundesausbildungsförderungsgesetz* or, more popularly, BaFöG is a federal scheme of student financial support, and there are also mechanisms of coordination between the higher education systems of the different states. But the main thrust of legislation and financial regulation is at the state level.

The basic *Diplom* qualification awarded by universities can officially be obtained after three years of study, but normally takes considerably longer. "As a rule eight to nine semesters of degree related studies and additional one to two examination semesters are necessary to acquire a *Diplom* degree at universities and university equivalent institutions. As such, the duration of studies is at least five to six years. In practice more time is usually required."[7] Subsequently, the *Magister* master's degree requires a further one to two years of study. German students normally enter the university at 19 years of age or even older, thus German graduates are in their late twenties at least before they are able to enter the labor market. This is several years older than their counterparts in many other European countries, especially Great Britain, and is a cause of some concern in German universities which fear the loss of students to other countries with the abolition of intra-European restrictions on student eligibility for financial support to study in other European Community countries.

The only form of financial support for students in Germany is loans provided under BaFöG. Even this is not generous, amounting to less than $1,000 per student per year at the beginning of the 1990s. Conversely, German students pay no fees and the constitution forbids universities to charge students for tuition.

British students conventionally enter full-time degree courses at the age of 17 in Scotland and 18 in England. The courses normally last for three years in England and four years in Scotland, but a few are longer, especially in engineering and medicine. In addition, a relatively generous system of student grants for full-time students, although limited to the prescribed length of courses recognized by the government, has done much to ensure that over 90% of students successfully complete their courses within the prescribed period. Thus, the typical British graduate enters the labor market at the age of 21 or 22, younger than in most other European countries. This early entry to the labor market sometimes raises doubts in other countries about whether a British degree in a subject such as engineering can really be the equivalent of a degree in a country where it may take twice as long to complete the course. The short answer is that up to the late 1980s when enrollment rates were considerably lower than in most other European countries, and expenditure per student much higher, British universities could almost certainly produce graduates of equivalent capability in a much shorter period. Since 1988, there has been a massive expansion with a much smaller increase in resources, so the question is now certainly a legitimate one with respect to a large number of the graduates now being produced. Furthermore, the government *is* encouraging universities to offer degrees after two years of intensive full-time study, which it is hoping to achieve by persuading some universities to use vacation periods for teaching. This trend is likely to accentuate the tendency for some universities to drop serious research altogether and to further doubts in other European countries about the real labor market value of a British first degree.

Amongst smaller European Community countries, the Netherlands, Belgium, Greece, Denmark, Ireland, Portugal, and even Luxembourg, with its one university and two other institutions, have well defined binary systems with a clear demarcation of function between the university and non-university sectors.

In Belgium, partly as a result of the political compromise on which the country is based, which results in separate French- and Flemish-speaking universities, higher education institutions have a high degree of institutional autonomy. Academically, the Belgian system has a broad resemblance to that of France, with three two-year cycles, the *Kandidaat*, the *Licentiaat*, and the *Doctoraat*.

Denmark more closely resembles Germany: the *kandidateksamen* is the most common university qualification and courses last from four to seven years. Following this, another four years are required for the *magisterkonferens* (master's) degree. As in Germany, government has a high degree of administrative control over the universities.

The Netherlands also has some resemblance to Germany in its course structures: the first degree in Dutch universities is the *doctoral* and the course normally takes five to six years. However, recent reforms have given Dutch universities legal and financial autonomy, but "an important condition for obtaining (government) funding is that the universities adhere to the national statutory regulations and conform to government systems of planning and funding."[8]

In Greece, first degree courses (called *Ptychia*) last four to five years. A singular feature of Greek higher education is the very large number of students studying in other countries, about 31,000 out of 200,000 in 1989.

In Ireland, degree courses normally last four years and the system has a structure very similar to that of the United Kingdom. The Portuguese system, with two levels of degree, the *bacharel*, awarded after three years of study at non-university institutions, and the *licenciado*, awarded after four to six years at a university, bears a considerable resemblance to that of Spain.

Significant fees are charged in Belgium (about $600), Ireland (about $2,000), and the Netherlands (about $900). No fees at all are paid in Denmark and Greece and fees in Portugal are minimal. Only in the Netherlands amongst this group of countries does a significant proportion of the income of higher education institutions (about 10%) come from any source other than general public subsidy of institutions.

Even though the 12 higher education systems of Western Europe can be reduced to four main categories—the British, French, German, and Spanish systems—according to dimensions of length and efficiency of first degree courses, degree of institutional autonomy, and mechanisms of finance, there are intrinsic problems in making general statements about any two of them.

Three performance indicators do have some reasonable validity in comparing European higher education systems with each other and with those of the United States.

- number of students who embark on a course of higher education expressed as a percentage of a standardized age group
- number who complete a first degree or equivalent course expressed as a percentage of a standardized age group
- percentage of gross national product devoted to higher education

These indicators for the latest available year in European Community countries and the United States are shown in Table 1.

Tables 1 to 3, together with the discussion of the previous section shows Spain, Italy, and Ireland with little non-degree higher education. Belgium, Denmark, France, Spain, and, above all, Italy have a much higher percentage of the population entering degree courses than emerging with the qualification. The big public spenders on higher education in relation to national income are Denmark, Ireland, and the Netherlands and the list is extended to include the U.K. and Germany if financial support to students and private expenditure are included. The United States devotes a far higher proportion of its national income to higher education than any European country. Although the tables do not show it explicitly because financial support for students and private finance of higher education institutions are combined, it

---

TABLE 1

EUROPEAN HIGHER EDUCATION PERFORMANCE INDICATORS

	Enrollments per 1,000 18-23 Popn	Expenditure per student as % GNP per head	Student years per Graduate	Expenditure per graduate as % GNP per head
U.K. 1992	26.0	.44	N/A	N/A
Spain	31.6	.35	3.79	1.33
Norway	34.6	.24	5.93	1.42
France	34.7	.24	5.93	1.42
Greece	27.2	.25	6.61	1.65
U.K. 1988	23.5	.49	3.77	1.85
Belgium	33.8	.33	5.92	1.95
Sweden	41.3	.35	5.62	1.97
Ireland	23.3	.58	3.74	2.17
Germany	32.2	.31	9.20	2.85
Switzerland	24.8	.42	7.43	3.12
Italy	26.3	.23	13.61	3.13
Finland	40.7	.39	8.79	3.43
U.S.A.	63.0	.53	7.00	3.60
Netherlands	33.0	.68	5.74	3.90
Portugal	17.6	.46	12.83	5.90
Denmark	30.6	.66	9.23	6.09

SOURCES: World Education Report 1991 UNESCO
            UNESCO Statistical Yearbook 1991
            UK 1992 derived from Government Expenditure Plans

TABLE 2

COMPARATIVE HIGHER EDUCATION PERFORMANCE INDICATORS 1988/89

	New Entrants as percentage of relevant age group		No. obtaining quali-fications as a % of relevant age group		Expenditure on H.E. as % of GDP 1988	
	sub-degree courses	degree courses	sub-degree courses	degree courses	Public #	Total ##
Belgium*	n/a	19.8	15.8	11.6	.87	.99
Denmark	15.5	27.6	10.3	10.1	1.14	1.58
France	13.3	23.1	14.7	12.1	.59	.67
Germany	9.2	19.5	7.7	13.3	.75	1.28
Ireland*	15.1	15.6	1.0	17.2	1.01	1.30
Netherlands#	18.3	12.3	16.5	11.4	1.22	2.03
Spain	<0.1	36.6	<0.1	17.0	.43	.56
U.K.	6.2	15.0	12.3	16.3	.63	1.27
United States	22.0	33.0	12.7	25.6	2.33	2.50

SOURCE: Entry and Graduation Rates: *Education at a Glance* OECD, 1989
Expenditure: *Public Expenditure on Higher Education*: F. Kaiser, J. Kingsley, London, 1992
Total Expenditure: ibid and *Financing Higher Education—Current Patterns*: G. Williams OECD, 1990

NOTES: *non-degree course entrants included with degree course entrants
#Includes only public expenditure on higher education institutions
##Total includes expenditure on student support and income from other sources including fees and income from industry.

TABLE 3

SOURCES OF INCOME OF EUROPEAN HIGHER EDUCATION INSTITUTIONS

			General Public Funds	Fees	Other Income
Finland	Public Institutions	1987	83.0%	–	15.0%
France	All Institutions	1984	89.5%	4.7%	5.8%
Germany	All Institutions	1986	68.5%	–	31.5%
Netherlands	All Institutions	1985	80.0%	12.0%	8.0%
Norway	Public Institutions	1987	90.0%	–	10.0%
Spain	Universities	Mid-1980s	80.0%	20.0%	n.a.
	Polytechnics	1986/87	72.4%	16.2%	11.4%
U.K.	Universities	1991			

NOTES: Finalnd: Norway: Figures for fees not available but very small
France: Expenditure of National Ministry of France
U.S.: Almost all the fees of U.K. undergraduate students are paid out of public funds. This amounts to about half the fee income of universities and probably a greater proportion of the fee income of polytechnics.

is worth noting that Great Britain, the Netherlands, Germany, and Denmark are EC countries with significant financial support for students, but only in Great Britain is this support predominantly in the form of grants, though it is in the process of changing into a loan-based system.

RECENT DEVELOPMENTS IN HIGHER EDUCATION FUNDING IN WESTERN EUROPE

Since about 1980, several European countries have experienced increased stringency in the public funds available to higher education and a shift from input based formulae towards output-oriented formulae and conditional grants and market incentives. These shifts have resulted in significant changes in the nature of higher education. In several countries, these changes in public funding have been accompanied by a search for alternative private sources of funds.

Many governments now see financial incentives as a more effective way of influencing the pattern of higher education than administrative intervention, which has previously been the most common form of government regulation in most of Europe. Public funding agencies are becoming increasingly selective; in several countries they are beginning to see their role as "buying" academic services on behalf of the community rather than managing or regulating academic institutions. In general, there is growing government interest in focusing public funds on what are perceived to be national needs. Changes under way in several countries include:

- increased sophistication of the formulae used in determining the allocations to institutions
- greater financial autonomy for the institutions once they have received their funds
- increased proportion of income from student fees
- sharper distinction between funding of research and of teaching
- increased proportion of public funding to be "bid for" by the institutions
- larger share of income from contracts with employers and commercial organizations[9]

The most important of these, in terms of the amount of resources involved, is the increasing use of output-based formula funding. Recent reforms in Denmark and the Netherlands are good examples of the use of formulae to provide sophisticated incentive systems.

In Denmark the resource allocation or budget model attempted to allocate university budgets into activity areas of the institutions as opposed to the previous practice where the institutions had received a total amount to be administered by the institutions themselves. By using a very fine meshed division into activity areas the central budget agency gets a fairly great influence on the budget of individual institutions. . . .it becomes possible for the central authorities to make considerable resource related priority decisions between the subject areas of the institutions. An interesting feature of the model is that resources are linked not to the number of students but to the number of students completing courses.[10]

This was an attempt to deal with a problem that Danish universities share with those of Germany and the Netherlands, the very long periods of study before students graduate, so payment of universities for completion of courses rather than for starting them provides an incentive for universities to see that students complete.

This shift of emphasis not surprisingly met with considerable opposition from the universities and subsequently the government has modified the scheme so that its interventions are at the margin rather than apparently over the whole of the expenditure of universities. The formula allocation remains, but each university is guaranteed as much as 99% of its previous income as core funds; additional incremental funds are made available to each institution selectively on the basis of criteria determined by the government. This "core plus margin" approach has subsequently been refined in the United Kingdom and it is discussed further in the next section.

The Netherlands' system of funding also consists essentially of formula-based block grants being paid to universities and other autonomous institutions. In that country too

an important feature is that funding is not based simply on enrollment. Instead the staffing and resources formulae provide strong incentives for a rapid selection of potential dropouts and the stimulation of rapid graduation. For every dropout and every graduate the institution receives a formula based amount of money that is independent of the real studying time of the students. There are also grants for specific purposes. Excluding (capital) investment these grants amount to 6% of the total allocation.[11]

Both these schemes illustrate the growing concern of European governments to reconcile the legitimate demands of academic institutions for sufficient autonomy to be able to carry out teaching and research according to academic and professional judgements with their responsibility for determining major priorities in the use of public funds. In the examples, both Denmark and the Netherlands are using the funding formula to encourage course completion.

The use of increasingly sophisticated formulae has clearly been facilitated by the expansion of computerized management models. However, in developing complex formulae one problem, referred to in both the Dutch and Danish reports to the OECD, is that complexity may distort the signals that the formulae are intended to convey.

In addition to the changes in core funding, an increasing number of governments believe that the private sector can bear some of the cost burden through student fees and contracts and donations from employers. Many countries have changed administrative regulations, and in some cases the legal status of higher education institutions, in order to allow them to retain earnings from research, consultancy, and the provision of full-cost courses. It is becoming recognized that unless this happens there is little incentive for academic staff to make the effort necessary to attract income from what are described in Germany as "third party sources." Another argument gaining ground among policy makers in several European countries is that since many of the benefits of higher education accrue to private individuals and to the enterprises that employ them, they should be prepared to meet some of the costs.

In several countries there is serious discussion of the possibility of charging fees to students as a way of contributing towards the cost of higher education. However, amongst European countries at present, only in the Netherlands, Spain, and the United Kingdom do fees constitute a significant percentage of the total income of higher education institutions, and in the United Kingdom fees for nearly all British undergraduate students are in fact paid out of public funds. In Germany and Greece, the payment of fees by first degree students is thought to breach the constitutional requirement that the state should provide higher education to all who show themselves likely to be able to benefit from it—which they do by passing the necessary secondary school examinations. On the other hand, in all European countries fees *are* charged for "continuing" or "recurrent" education of adults, and in most of them this university activity has grown rapidly during the past decade for financial as well as broader economic and social reasons.

There is some concern within European universities over what are seen by many academics as the damaging effects of these changes. Not all of this concern is the special pleading of an interest group that is having its privileges reduced. One particular worry in countries accustomed to fairly homogeneous national university systems is that plural funding increases financial and, subsequently, academic disparities between universities. Concern has also been expressed that new forms of selective resource allocation formulae are resulting in excessive amounts of academic staff time being devoted to preparing proposals and accounting for the way in which funds are used. Another fear is that if core sources of funds are fully utilized in maintaining basic activities, then the only finance for innovation comes from subsidiary sources of funds. This may give such sources an influence on the patterns of the development of higher education disproportionate to the amount of resources they actually contribute.

CHANGES IN HIGHER EDUCATION FUNDING IN GREAT BRITAIN DURING THE 1980s AND 1990s

Contrary to many claims by British academics, the 1980s were a period of modest growth in resources for British higher education. However, the sources of funds, the channels through which they became available to universities, and the activities for which they were used, changed considerably. There was a shift away from incremental and loosely monitored formula funding by a single government agency towards more closely specified formulae and contractual funding by a wider variety of public and private funding bodies. Table 4 shows the changes in the amount and composition of the recurrent income of universities over the 1980s. Regular public expenditure per student went down by 10% and the percentage of income that came in the form of a core grant from government declined from 65% to 48%.

TABLE 4

CHANGES IN THE SOURCES OF INCOME OF BRITISH UNIVERSITIES 1982/83 TO 1989/90

	1982/83	1989/90
General grants	65.2	48.4
Fees	12.9	13.9
Research grants from industry	1.4	2.1
Other research grants	12.2	16.8
"Short" (full course) costs	0.8	1.9
Gifts	1.0	3.3
Other	6.1	13.6
Total at constant prices: (1982 = 100)	100	129
Per Student	100	114
General grant + fee per student	100	90

These changes have had a marked effect on the nature of management in British universities. Until the 1980s, block grant allocations from the University Grants Committee reinforced the central authority of universities. Resources were allocated to the institution and this gave its central management the dominant influence on their internal allocation. In effect the central management of the university bought services from the academic departments.

When income is derived from many sources, and takes the form of payment for services rendered, resource allocation and financial management are more complex. In effect, the academic departments in many universities are now buying services from the center. There has been a marked change from administrative allocation and regulation towards more varied systems of institutional resource allocation and financial management, involving priorities, incentives, levies, systematic management information, and cost analysis. These changes have sometimes led to centralized structures in which institutional leaders can marshal resources very quickly, but the need to provide incentives has more often resulted in the devolution of many responsibilities to subsidiary management units. Some universities now resemble franchising operations in which the central authority imposes a levy on departmental franchisees in return for the provision of central services and an easily recognisable corporate image.

Budgetary devolution and financial responsibility are replacing the participatory academic decision-making structures that were the dominant characteristic of higher education management in Great Britain in the 1960s and 1970s. Whether this democracy of the social market is an adequate replacement for, or preferable to, the democracy of the debating chamber is not simply an economic issue. However, from the economic viewpoint, there have been considerable apparent increases in the efficiency of teaching in terms of output per unit of input. Average expenditure per student in universities fell by 10% between 1982/83 and 1989/90, but, the number of graduates rose by 10%. At the same time, the proportion obtaining first class honors degrees rose from 6% to 8.3%; the number of higher degrees rose by 60% and the number of Ph.D.s by over 34%.

Income generation from the sale of teaching and research services became a major activity of many British universities during the past decade. The costing and pricing of income generating activities are creating tensions, sometimes severe, between academic departments and central administration. Most members of staff claim that they undertake contract research either because it is academically worthwhile in itself, or because it generates income that enables them to do work that is worthwhile. Institutional managers are more concerned with the question of how the full costs of all activities are to be met and are beginning to insist that all supplementary activities are fully costed and make a proper contribution to institutional overhead costs. However, the issue of appropriate costing of indirect resource use is a matter of lively debate. Many university finance officers believe that at present external funding brings little net income because services are underpriced. Some argue that this is why many academic institutions are in financial trouble despite staff claims about being overworked—all their products are underpriced. In the past, government core funding has effectively financed the cost of bidding for other initiatives and has underwritten the other activities of universities and polytechnics. Reduced core government funding is making this less possible. Most universities and polytechnics have begun to develop standard formulae for pricing externally funded activities and for allocating the proceeds between individuals, cost centers, and central services. The average contribution made by university research contracts to institutional overheads increased from 9% in 1984 to 13% in 1989. However, when substantial contributions to the overhead expenditures of the university are recovered, academics who have earned them often resent the surpluses going to what they see as unnecessary central administration or the subsidy of less active departments.

On the other hand, the use of financial incentives for individual members of staff is growing. Most universities and polytechnics now have some system of rewards for staff who generate supplementary income. In itself this is of little economic importance. It is essentially a market adjustment to a situation in which national salary scales operate but different specialisms have widely different employment opportunities outside higher education.[12] However, the widespread payment of what are in effect commissions is often seen as another departure from the traditional collegiality of the British university.

Further tensions arise as a result of the growing numbers of staff employed on income generating activities. There is much confusion over whether their work is now part of the mainstream business of the academic institution, or whether they are essentially an academic proletariat whose function is to generate a surplus to give established teaching and research staff the time to carry out real academic work. The proportion of such staff rose from 22% of all academic staff in 1980 to 36% in 1989/90; the conditions of employment of staff on this kind of contract are considerably less favorable than those of established academic staff.

In addition to the staff employed on short-term contracts, most universities now have a centralized institutional consultancy service that employs its own staff. Many of these companies are in the area of computer software and biotechnology. Consultancy is normally undertaken primarily for financial gain, but it is also justified in terms of opportunities for practical professional experience for academic staff or students, and as a promotional activity to attract subsequent research contracts.

The science park is the most ambitious and highly organized of the forms of external income generation and industry-higher education collaboration that developed during the 1980s. About half of British universities now have some property development that they describe as a science park. However, the pressure to use science park facilities to full capacity has, in many cases, led to dilution of the original concept; many have evolved into more general business parks that are little more than commercial developments on rather attractive sites. In some later developments, speculative building was a prominent feature followed, as boom gave way to recession in the 1990s, by problems of under-utilization. Few British university science parks have yet made a profit.

British higher education institutions of the 1990s are behaving as multi-product firms with a portfolio of activities determined by the cost of inputs and the changing market conditions for each product range. The production function is complex; some activities are complementary with each other and some competitive and many are both complementary and competitive. Changes in funding are altering the composition of academic activities and the balance between academic and supporting activities.

INITIATIVES OF THE EUROPEAN COMMUNITY

Higher education has not so far been a major priority of the European Community, but there are two areas in which the EC has been active: harmonization of professional qualifications, and promotion of staff and student mobility programs. In December 1991, the Commission published for discussion a policy *Memorandum on Higher Education in the European Community*, which summarizes progress so far and makes proposals for future developments.

Given the variety of university qualifications outlined in the first section of this essay, harmonization is no easy task, and Europe has so far made little attempt to secure common structures of higher education courses in different countries. One reason is that rather like the federal government in the United States, the authorities of the Community are not allowed to be directly involved in education. Their aim so far has been to promote acceptance of professional qualifications throughout the Community so that doctors, lawyers, engineers, and other professionals with qualifications from one European country can practice throughout the Community. This aim must be achieved if member states are to comply with the treaty requirement that from January 1, 1993, there should be free movement of labor throughout the Community.

A Directive from the Ministerial Council of the Community requires a "general system for the recognition of higher education diplomas awarded on completion of professional education and training of at least three years' duration." Working parties from professional bodies have spent several years attempting to satisfy themselves that an English engineering degree obtained in three years study is the equivalent of a German or Dutch degree that takes twice that time to obtain. In fact, they have decided that it cannot, and the British government has now agreed to fund a substantial number of "premium" four-year engineering degree schemes. There has been no analogous problem in medicine, since British medical courses already last six years.

The Commission has established a network of National Academic Recognition Centers (NARIC), a system of nationally designated units whose purpose is to provide employers (as well as students and their higher education institutions) with authoritative information on the value and recognition of educational credentials obtained in other countries. The 1991 *Memorandum* goes a good deal further and points out that "The free movement of persons and the recognition of qualifications for professional purposes create, in effect, a single labor market for the categories of person concerned and this clearly has implications both for the supply of and the demand for highly qualified personnel." However, it would not be unfair to summarize all this effort in the area of equivalence of qualifications by saying that it so far has consisted largely of exhortation backed up by a certain amount of case law in the European Courts. There is still a long way to go before it can be claimed that Europe is really a single labor market for highly qualified workers.

Student and staff mobility has also received considerable attention from a wide range of programs. The largest and most widely known is the European Community Action Scheme for the Mobility of University Students (ERASMUS), which, despite its name, provides for mobility of both staff and students. ERASMUS is essentially a Community-funded scheme that pays the living costs of students who do at least one unit of their courses in a country other than their own. Staff exchanges to develop links between individual institutions are also encouraged. The scheme is intended to consist mainly of bilateral or multilateral exchange schemes between two or more institutions, so institutional costs are self-balancing, but in practice some geographical imbalance exists.

Other student mobility programs include TEMPUS (Trans European Mobility Scheme for University Studies), the essential purpose of which is to provide opportunities for students from Eastern Europe to take some courses in a university in Western Europe. This scheme also intends an element of reciprocity, but in practice most traffic is one way.

NOTES

1. See Frans Kaiser et al., *Public Expenditure on Higher Education: A Comparative Study in the Member States of the European Community*. (London: Jessica Kingsley, 1992).

2. Kaiser et al., op. cit.

3. In the national research assessment exercise announced in December 1992, the average score of the newly designated universities indicated a performance in research below a level defined as "research quality that equates to attainable levels of national (as opposed to international) excellence in up to half of the subareas of activity." Universities Funding Council, *Research Assessment Exercise 1992: The Outcome*, Circular 26/92, Universities Funding Council, Bristol.

4. Anita van Resandt, ed., *A Guide to Higher Education Systems in the European Community* (London: Kogan Page, 1991).
5. *ibid.*
6. Kaiser et al., op. cit.
7. van Resandt, op. cit.
8. Kaiser et al., op. cit.
9. G.L. Williams, *Financing Higher Education: Current Patterns* (OECD, 1990).
10. Organization for Economic Cooperation and Development, *Changing Patterns of Finance in Higher Education—Case Study: Denmark* (OECD, 1988).
11. Organization for Economic Cooperation and Development, *Changing Patterns of Finance in Higher Education—Case Study: The Netherlands* (OECD, 1988).
12. G.L. Williams, T. Blackstone, and D. Metcalfe, *The Academic Labor Market* (Amsterdam: Elsevier, 1974).

ADDITIONAL RESOURCES

Clark, B.R. *The Higher Education System: Academic Organization in Cross-National Perspective.* Berkeley: University of California Press, 1983.

Committee of Vice-Chancellors and Principals. *The Costing of Research Projects in Universities: A Report and Guidance to Universities.* London: C.V.C.P., 1988.

Garvin, D.A. *The Economics of University Behaviour.* New York: Academic Press, 1981.

Williams, B.R. *The Effects of the New Funding Mechanisms in Universities.* London: Center for Higher Education Studies, 1991.

Williams, G.L. *Changing Patterns of Finance in Higher Education.* Open University Press, 1992.

Williams, G.L., Woodhall, M., and O'Brien, U. *Overseas Students and Their Place of Study.* London: Overseas Students Trust, 1986.

Globalization of Knowledge

* * * * * * * *

Steven Muller

EXECUTIVE SUMMARY

How can American higher education institutions expect to be affected by the "globalization of knowledge," or the international flows of intellectual capital? American institutions of higher education have long been recognized as leaders in the knowledge industry, both nationally and internationally, according to Steven Muller. Consequently, the current information age could be termed a "golden age" for American higher education and our institutions should be not only be leaders, but beneficiaries in the information age. Muller discusses four issues related to globalization and how their resolutions will determine how higher education adapts to the international challenges presented by the information age.

The first issue is how universities will access and manage the international flow of knowledge. Muller suggests that participating in a consortial arrangement would be the most beneficial scenario, with institutional libraries playing a central role. Faculty members would be key to this type of scenario. They would be expected to at least be aware of most foreign source material, but would they be willing to donate the time and energy required to do this? A second issue to be considered involves possible future restrictions on information sharing in order to protect national interests. The United States was once a leader in science and technol-

ogy innovations. American research universities are now being looked upon as a force to bring some of this prestige back to America. Muller suggests a third important concern: the information age may widen gaps that already exist between the "haves and have-nots on the globe." Developed countries are expected to reap tremendous benefits from the increased availability of knowledge; but will less developed countries be left out in the cold? Even the United States is expected to have a whole class of citizens who will be "dysfunctional in the information society." How will higher education institutions ensure that everyone is able to take advantage of the opportunities provided by the information age? Finally, Muller addresses the problem of whether globalizing international capital will assist or hinder the university in "integrative conceptualization."

INTRODUCTION

The scientific and technological explosion of the latter half of the twentieth century has vastly increased the store of human knowledge and made that knowledge much more accessible. Over a spectrum ranging from the micro to the macro scale, the human ability to identify, analyze, measure, manipulate, understand, and predict the behavior of matter in the universe now greatly exceeds all such human achievement of the past. Simultaneously, the human capacity to communicate knowledge universally, and almost instantly, has exploded at a rate comparable to the explosion of knowledge itself. Furthermore, the explosion of both human knowledge and communication continues unabated and is likely to produce further capabilities beyond imagination. Computers, electron microscopes, scanners, satellites, fiber-optics, nuclear magnetic resonance imaging, and a whole litany of technologies are transforming the landscape of human understanding and interaction.

Knowledge is power. That ancient truism means that those who possess relevant knowledge have a better capacity than those who lack it to move matter—or matters—to their benefit. In days past, those who wielded power in human societies and wished to retain their hold on power usually tried their best to limit the spread of knowledge. Libraries in China, for example, were accessible only to the Mandarins. In our day, however, technologically advanced societies are already almost totally dependent on pervasive applications of technology, for whose production and operation knowledge is required.

In these societies, therefore, knowledge must of necessity be widely disseminated and is therefore more difficult to restrict. For example, because computer literacy has become necessary for more and more of those employed in society, knowledge accessible to the computer cannot easily be limited strictly and exclusively to only what is necessary for an employee. Not so long ago, the Soviet Union refused to make available either street maps of its cities or public telephone directories. Then the competitive demands of advanced technology required Soviet citizens to have access to more and more knowledge to remain functional. Such expansion of the knowledge base contributed to the need for Glasnost—more openness—which in turn contributed to the disintegration of Soviet totalitarianism.

The present stage of technologically advanced societies is appropriately labeled the information age. The phrase captures both the extent to which more and more information exists, and the ability to share that information widely and rapidly. It seems equally appropriate to speak of the knowledge industry, with reference to those enterprises engaged in or closely related to both the advancement and dissemination of human knowledge. It is reasonable to assume—if knowledge indeed is power—that the knowledge industry is powerful in societies of the information age. Certainly there is plenty of evidence that efficient for-profit components of the knowledge industry are highly lucrative, albeit also savagely competitive. It is also possible to describe humanity's still rapidly accumulating wealth of new knowledge as intellectual capital. This image conveys the concept that knowledge is a commodity that can be manufactured, bought, and sold. As such a commodity, knowledge becomes the most essential, and therefore most highly prized, commercial product of the information age. Humanity's accumulation of knowledge, described as intellectual capital, has hugely grown and is still expanding. The expectation follows that, properly invested or applied, this new wealth of knowledge will enormously enrich the human condition.

A final obvious observation is that geographic distance, national borders, and—at least to some degree—even language barriers no longer present significant obstacles to the international movement of intellectual capital, especially to the instantaneous communication of data. If there is indeed a marketplace for intellectual capital, that marketplace is truly global and appears to be extending into space as well. While the nation-state remains the standard form of large-scale human social organization, it has already been substantially eroded by the commercial and financial markets. With the end of the Cold War, the advanced technological societies of the information age seem to be well on the road toward a single global marketplace of ideas, data, and communication.

Indisputably, higher education is positioned at the very heart of the knowledge industry in the information age. The modern university's research and teaching mission is a central component of the advancement and communication of knowledge. The question, then, is how higher education is likely to be affected by the international and multinational flows of intellectual capital. As yet, that question has no definitive answer, nor will such an answer be offered here, but it has generally been assumed that the international dimension of the information age will be particularly benign and agreeable for higher education. Ever since the Western university first took form a millennium ago, the very name "university" has been linked to the concept of "universitas," the universal nature of knowledge and scholarship. Universities in general have always been open to ideas, information, teachers, and students from other societies. It seems logical to anticipate that the information age overall will be a golden age for higher education and that the accelerated and all-embracing international flows of intellectual capital will be uniquely congenial and rewarding for universities. Such anticipation may well turn out to be justified. If so, then American higher education's leadership in the knowledge industry, both nationally and internationally, should allow it to continue as a leader and emerge as a primary beneficiary as well. However, at least four issues arise for further consideration, and their eventual resolution will shape the way in which American higher education adapts to the international dimension of the information age.

ACCESSING AND MANAGING THE INTERNATIONAL FLOW OF KNOWLEDGE

The first issue focusses on the ability of American higher education to access and manage the international flow of knowledge in the information age. This issue does not raise large or dramatic questions. Instead it represents a mosaic of the prosaic. For instance, how does one balance the need of students and faculty to have access to informational material—books, journals, newspapers, films, tapes, and electronically based data—from all over the world against the viability of any single university or college—no matter how wealthy or large—to access and store all of this material? The answer clearly lies in institutional participation in consortia that will identify, collect, assemble, and organize such informational material for access by their subscribers. It is highly unlikely that any one consortium would ever emerge that could accomplish this whole task for all of American higher education. More likely, a combination of regional or specialized consortia will continue to evolve from the substantial base that already exists.

A question that in part derives from, and is at least linked to, the consortium approach to accessing international informational material involves the future nature of the college or university library. Most likely the cost of consortia participations will become institutionally centralized in the library, rather than scattered widely throughout individual college and university departments. Such institutional centralization also will presumably characterize operational interaction between subscriber and consortium: the informational material available through the consortium will be accessible to the institution through the library. Increasingly over time, however, that material will not consist of books. Even books themselves are apt to be accessed via computerized readers rather than delivered on loan to an institutional subscriber. What then will be the role of the college or university library in this international context over the decades ahead? On most campuses the library is already well along in the transition from a repository of books and journals to an information center linked to networks both external and internal to the institution. If, for example, not only films and tapes from all over the world but also live specialized programming via satellite through consortial arrangements become available, the demand is almost certain to arise that the library manage the whole range of the facilities on campus which are involved in the process of access and use of data from off-campus locations. All this suggests that the prosaic question of effective management of the international flow of intellectual capital represents a serious, major problem for the American college and university.

Another set of questions arises concerning the involvement and education of college and university faculty in the use of the entire range of informational material from foreign lands. Students themselves cannot as a rule be expected to identify foreign sources on their own. They require and are entitled to faculty guidance, which in turn depends on faculty familiarity with, or at least awareness of, foreign source material. Lack of faculty diligence in cultivating the full international knowledge base of their own field for both themselves and their students would obviously inhibit their full ability to draw on the global store of intellectual capital. As is generally true in American higher education, responsibility for such diligence is vested primarily in each faculty member. Individual faculty diligence is susceptible to institutional encouragement but almost never to institutional policing and enforcement. In this connection, it is interesting to note that 11 years ago a small group of American and European research universities joined in a consortium designed to enable researchers to engage in live, real-time international interchanges via satellite telecasting. While the consortium still exists and has done occasional programming, faculty participation at all of the institutions involved has been minimal, primarily because the need for live, real-time international interchange was perceived to be almost nonexistent. The obvious lesson to be drawn is that institutional arrangements for international information exchange will prove effective only to the extent to which they are actively supported by faculty.

These matters become exquisitely complicated when one realizes how much change humanity and human institutions have already accommodated over an extremely short time span. Persons now in their sixties reached maturity before there were computers, network television, satellites, or optic fibers. They are adjusting to technological innovation that makes international informational material potentially available on a scale undreamed of when they entered professional life. The generations that follow will have to keep on adjusting—to such things as computerized translations of foreign language materials and all kinds of new compendia of data and material—to the point where analysis of what is available may become a full-time activity in itself. Aside from the sheer human strain of constant adaptation to innovation, there will also be questions of constantly mounting costs and priorities. While there is little doubt that almost any range of data, publications, and other informational material from all over the world can be rendered accessible on a timely basis almost anywhere in American higher education at a price, what will that price be, and how affordable will it seem? What priority will professors, deans, and other administrators give to the international dimension of research and teaching when the cost of participation in various consortia has to be balanced against a host of competing claims for limited dollars? A possible irony here is that electronic communication transcends geography to the point where a single professor at a small college can in theory have access to all the informational resources from abroad that are available to his or her several colleagues at the nearest major research university. In theory, yes— but will that professor's small college make the resource available to permit him or her in fact to tap into the full range of available resources? And will that professor—or for that matter, any professor—be able and willing to muster the time and energy required to master the worldwide wealth of constantly and currently available information? There is, in summary, no doubt that a rich and full range of international informational material will be available to American higher education. However, effective communication still requires not only a sender but a receiver. The ability to use an international database will depend on the will to do so, and the priority assigned to that will, primarily by faculty.

RESTRICTIONS ON OPEN SHARING OF INFORMATION

A second major issue, which raises more dramatic questions, involves the restrictions on open sharing of information by universities on an international basis in order to protect commercial or national interests. This issue is complex, and past experience does not provide definitive guidance. Sponsored research on a large scale in American universities really began only during the Second World War, and grew enormously in the Cold War era.

During World War II, the government turned to a few American universities to devise answers to national security problems, including development of the proximity fuse, rocket delivery systems, more accurate and sophisticated radar, and—best known of all—the atomic bomb. Prior to these efforts and, of course, prior to the era of "big science," neither large-scale research nor large-scale research sponsorship was in evidence on the American university scene. After the end of World War II, however, large-scale university research with large-scale federal sponsorship not only continued but greatly increased, and at an ever accelerating pace. Inspired by successful research to win the war, government in part sought to address health problems by "making war" on several diseases—war conducted under the aegis of the newly founded National Institutes of Health and actually waged mostly in university laboratories. In even larger part, however, the Cold War effort replaced World War II as the cause and motivator for enormous new national security research initiatives. The American university community, which had been mobilized in research terms to win World War II, in effect remained mobilized to win the Cold War as well.

In wartime, there is a real and immediate enemy who presents a real threat. Giving aid and comfort to the enemy is an act of treason. Accordingly, it was an accepted part of the game that federally sponsored research to assist the war effort could and should be classified as secret and should be kept secret. This went wholly against the grain of the spirit of the university community, which had been wholly committed to freedom of teaching and research, was opposed to all efforts to restrict freedom to publish, and consistently and vigorously advocated totally open scholarship. Nevertheless, an exception to normal university practice was knowingly made during World War II for the sake of the war effort. That exception was partially continued during the Cold War period, but in the form of newly evolved institutional arrangements. "Classified" research—i.e., research classified secret—was generally banned from the teaching campus but permitted in separate facilities, located at university laboratories operated specifically to carry out national security research. Furthermore, individual university researchers were proscribed from doing classified research on campus, but were free to participate in classified research in off-campus settings—their own university's government-sponsored laboratory or a government facility. As a result, the American research university has had experience for nearly a half century with restrictions on the openness of research, all in the context of war or the Cold War, all related to the interests of national security, but generally not recently enforced on university teaching campuses. Because the Cold War has only just ended, and with such unexpected suddenness, and because its lasting aftermath still remains so uncertain, secrecy of research under university auspices in the interest of national security continues at this time, and it is by no means clear that it will cease or, if so, when or how.

In the meantime, the knowledge industry and the information age have assumed their present form. The explosion of science and technology has occurred over a whole range of technologically advanced societies. In its wake, the economy of the United States has become global and has not for some time been autarchically self-contained, as it was for most of the previous two centuries. At the same time, the United States no longer possesses the near monopoly on new science and technology that it enjoyed for the first two decades after World War II. Increasingly, American society has begun to look at the American research university as the needed driving force of a required economic regeneration of the United States. American industry, parts of which learned to work closely with university scientists as collaborators in national security research, has greatly increased its sponsorship of university research in areas of direct industrial relevance. Inevitably, questions of proprietary secrecy to protect future profitability of the results of research have arisen. True to the tradition of openness, however, universities have successfully insisted that industry-sponsored university research remain open. Products and techniques arising from or relevant to industry-sponsored university research can of course be patented; and the slowness of peer-reviewed publication usually means that a patent has been granted before the actual publication of a new product, device, or technique. Also, universities permit their researchers to observe proprietary secrecy when they work off-campus in industrial facilities; and a number of universities have created research parks that encourage industry to locate facilities close to campuses so as to encourage industry-university collaboration to the greatest extent possible short of moving university research to an industrial site or bringing industrial research directly on campus.

Industry-university collaboration serves a number of useful purposes. For the university, it offers opportunity to transfer the results of basic research into the mainstream of industrial development where new products are brought to market. Rapid transition from laboratory to new product is in the public interest, and it can, of course, be of special benefit to the university if a university patent is part of the creation of a successful new product. It is certainly true that universities look to industrial research support at the very least to supplement government research sponsorship, and also to support areas of research that have not proven capable of attracting sufficient support from government. Industry, of course, depends on university basic research as a principal source of new ideas, technologies, and potential new products, and also for the highly trained talent to which industry looks for its own personnel needs. These benign motives tend to be mutually supportive, and they go hand-in-hand with the globalism of the marketplace and the information society, insofar as both industrial corporations and major research universities have equivalent multi-national or international interests. There is, however, the risk in such arrangements that the incentives for and emphasis on applied research may, over time, erode the university's commitment to basic research. The effects of an academic reward system that encourages research rather than teaching have already been evident for several decades. A reward system with a clear preference for applied research is likely to prove equally effective. This risk will be magnified if government joins industry in treating major research universities primarily as engines for achieving American industrial renewal and innovation. In the post-Cold War era, it is more than possible that the national interest will be perceived far more in economic than in military terms, and that national security concerns and strategy will concentrate heavily on the nation's position in the international marketplace. Other nations—Germany, Japan, Great Britain, and France, for example—have long had national economic development goals as part of both domestic and foreign policy. In the past, the United States has neither consistently nor vigorously concentrated on such policy, mostly because the essentially self-contained size and strength of the American economy seemed to make it unnecessary, but also because the decentralization and freedom of the American market argued against centralized planning and direction.

Here again, however, the context of war—both the Second World War and the Cold War—engendered exceptions regarded as fully justifiable. The export of strategic materials to "the enemy" was prohibited, planned efforts were made to protect access to strategic raw materials from abroad, a number of domestic capabilities were subsidized so that they would remain available if needed for national security purposes, and both military and commercial sales or assistance abroad were planned and carried out as part of national security strategy. As noted, university research for national security purposes is often classified and therefore not shared with the international scientific community.

The United States may now develop a new or expanded national security policy, which will not only focus on international economic competition as a key priority, but will be fully conscious of the information society and will therefore concentrate on the knowledge industry. The impact of such a policy could not only create strong incentives for applied research in universities but also restrict scholarly publication and communication so as to preserve new science and technology as an exclusive national economic asset and to deny access to foreign competitors. Such a policy might seem little more than a logical extension of traditional national security policy and would be supported not merely by patriotism but by the full power and funding of the federal government. Major research universities would continue to be supported as indispensable national assets, but the price they would have to pay for their new place of power in the knowledge industry could be severe limitation of their freedom to communicate openly on an international basis. It would surely be ironic if humanity's new opportunity to build intellectual capital on a global basis were in this way undercut and reduced to competitive parochialism. Therefore, it may not be too soon for a vigorous effort to assure that the principles of free trade and open communication internationally apply fully in the information age, and to the knowledge industry.

THE GAP IN INFORMATION ACCESS

A third major issue arises with the prospect that the information age is likely to widen the gap between the haves and the have-nots on the globe. The proportionate disadvantage of those who lack access to and use of information and communications will become enormous. This problem involves both access to the technology of information and communication and to the learned skills to make access usable. The international dimension of this problem relates to the less developed societies, but there is also a domestic dimension that relates to the unschooled.

Knowledge alone, and information technology, do not suffice to produce societal development. As long as the required resources are lacking and as long as patterns of social organization remain counterproductive, modernization and technological development will continue to lag in many parts of the world. Scholars from less developed countries will continue to participate in American higher education, but their ability to employ their knowledge at home upon their return will remain limited to the level of progress of national development. Some of these scholars are as likely as were their predecessors to wish to remain permanently in highly developed settings where they can more fully put their skills to effective use. At least in the short run, the main international impact of the information age on the less developed societies is that their internal state of affairs will now be instantly and more clearly visible to a global audience. As a result, poverty and misery are no longer out of sight nor out of mind, but they persist nonetheless. There is deplorably little reason to hope that American colleges and universities have it within their power to lead the modernization of the less developed lands. They can continue—as they have been doing—to furnish knowledge and technology and to help train intellectual elites, but destitution, corruption, and civil strife have too long and too often undercut even such minimal assistance.

The better news is that communications technology now makes it possible to reach out into even the most remote countryside, so that theoretically even peasant farmers in tiny hamlets have access to and can be contacted with knowledge and information. At least to some degree, this is happening, for instance, in the People's Republic of China. However, a real interest on the part of this audience cannot be taken for granted nor even assumed, particularly because there are such obvious limits to the use they are able to make of the knowledge that reaches them. However, the potential is there, and there is hope that the time will soon come when the whole of humanity can share in the world's knowledge capital and communications system.

At this point, we must at least to mention the discouraging and ominous state of the gap that exists in the United States between the majority of Americans who participate in the information society, and the significant and growing minority that largely ignores it. Very briefly summarized, by the end of this decade approximately two of every five Americans will be African American, Hispanic American, Asian American, or Native American. While Asian Americans generally appear to adjust rapidly to the highly developed technological society of the United States, and while Native Americans largely continue to live on reservations in conditions that represent a national disgrace, the great majority of African Americans and Hispanic Americans are increasingly concentrated in urban ghettos throughout the country. While the urban environment theoretically offers them ready access to schooling and to the domestic communications system, all surveys reveal the extent to which these groups, particularly young African-American males, drop out of inner-city schools. It is also evident that many of them do not participate with respect either to reading materials or to much of network and cable television, although many of them do participate in computer games and other portions of entertainment technology, such as films and videos.

It is not appropriate here to digress into substantive analysis of this situation, except to note that it is clearly possible for some members of society to be fully aware of and have access to highly advanced communications technology and nevertheless almost wholly abstain from its knowledge component. The result of this phenomenon is a minority population that is essentially dysfunctional in the information society. Historic social divisions within national societies were most often based on economic status. In the information age, lack of knowledge may become equated with very low economic status, and thus give added definition to the concept of an underclass. The international dimension of this particular phenomenon is the replication outside the United States of similar urban ghettos within other highly advanced technological societies. It is far from clear whether whole parts of the world may perhaps replicate this phenomenon, remaining unaffected by knowledge even when they are tied into a global communications system.

As far as American higher education is concerned, colleges and universities are dependent on prior schooling for their students, but play no really significant role in the conduct of schooling, either domestically or internationally. There have been and surely will continue to be programs within higher education to reach out to persons of talent who have been educationally disadvantaged with respect to schooling. Most of these programs in the

United States are domestic, although a few, such as the Peace Corps, have reached abroad as well. No matter how praiseworthy such programs are, they do not even approach a solution, either to the problem of assuring schooling for all Americans that would qualify them for effective participation in the information society, or for achieving a similar goal on an international basis.

GLOBALIZING INTELLECTUAL CAPITAL

The last, and perhaps largest, issue related to the internationalization of knowledge asks whether globalizing intellectual capital will assist or hinder the university in its greatest task—integrative conceptualization. The effect to date of the knowledge explosion clearly has been to foster fragmentation and specialization rather than integration of knowledge. As more and more information becomes more and more readily available, mastery of information becomes an ever more challenging task. The challenge is most easily met when attention can be focussed only on the array of data bearing on a particular problem. Inevitably this involves a high degree of intellectual compartmentalization. Already, the sum of human knowledge cannot possibly be commanded by any single human mind. Instead, clusters of knowledge become the province of clusters of specialists, whose shared but narrow knowledge is paradoxically harder to share with nonspecialists to the very degree that it is most detailed and acute. This is an old and familiar phenomenon, complicated now only by the accelerating volume of data and number of specialized clusters of knowledge. More and more, the forest is no longer visible as each tree becomes a separate universe of knowledge.

Throughout its growth over a thousand years, a central mission of the university as an institution has been to enable individuals to acquire a foundation of knowledge sufficient both for general understanding and, as desired, for further selective specialization. The knowledge explosion has produced a situation in which it is no longer possible for single minds both to absorb and retain over a limited period of study all the facts that would constitute such a foundation. However, absorption and retention of a body of basic facts would prove to be futile in any case, even were it possible. Within a decade or two after the period of study the relevant facts will have been significantly amended and amplified. Happily, current information technology enables the individual mind to call on all of the relevant facts as needed, register and become aware of amendments and additions on a continuing basis, and thus command a range of facts far beyond unassisted individual recall. Unhappily, higher teaching has tended to lag behind higher learning, and all too often still emphasizes factual knowledge per se rather than the conceptual foundation that renders the facts useful and meaningful.

True globalization of knowledge has the potential to assist the provision of integrated rather than fragmented learning. Internationalization provides the possibility of an array of new perspectives that might virtually demand integration. Alternatively, the diversity of internationalization might simply add further to specialization, compartmentalization, and fragmentation. In this connection it is discouraging to note that to date the addition of new perspectives to the American curriculum has taken primarily the latter form—as in women's studies, African-American studies, gay studies, Native American studies—rather than resulting in revised and newly integrated approaches. International communication by itself does not mean international understanding. A global storehouse of intellectual capital could quite possibly constitute a Tower of Babel more easily than a true treasure-trove of worldwide enlightenment. It is the task of higher education throughout the world to achieve the latter and not settle for the Tower of Babel. Humanity's hope for the future lies in the prospect of a global civilization for which the tools are now at hand.

Any civilization is based on a set of commonly shared values, assumptions, and patterns of order. It must, in other words, be rooted solidly in some fundamental concepts. These concepts need not only to be developed but learned, over and over again, as they pass from one generation to the next. A global civilization in the information age runs the risk of being trivialized by horizontalization—the whole world can be too much with us on the surface, without depth and perspective. The task of higher education is not only to advance knowledge and to train specialists, but also to transmit civilization and to build a common foundation of learning. Human minds have for ages relied on supplements to memory, largely by means of books and other printed matter. Now the volume of knowledge is becoming ever greater, but the aids to memory have grown right along with it. However, we still need to know what data we wish to retrieve, and for what purpose, and we also need to know how to relate that data to other data so as to keep some sense of order and coherence. So the greatest task of higher learning is to achieve an ongoing re-integration of the ever advancing state of knowledge, and to do so on a global basis. Current headlines are a grim reminder that parochialism and xenophobia remain as strong as ever. We are far as yet from the concept of humanity as a single tribe, and the global village as the all-embracing super-parochial parish. Integration must take place in the mind before it can take effect in behavior. Knowledge as a product is the province of industry. Knowledge as a weapon has traditionally been the province of government. Knowledge as understanding is the province of the university, and as of now knowledge has outrun understanding by far. Higher learning must now restore understanding. With the tools at hand and the world no longer split into two armed camps, higher learning can and must strive at long last for global understanding.

Technological Change and the University: Impacts and Opportunities from Global Change

✻ ✻ ✻ ✻ ✻ ✻ ✻

Lewis Branscomb

EXECUTIVE SUMMARY

According to Lewis Branscomb, American universities are not using the technology that they create as effectively as they should to carry out their primary mission—the education of undergraduate students. One exception to this has been the lead role that universities have played in the proliferation of computer networks, such as Internet; universities will also be influential players in the future of the National Research and Education Network, which will link universities with industrial and government labs. However, Branscomb points out that other innovations in information technology also provide great promise to higher education institutions. These innovations include computer-assisted learning, which could increase faculty productivity and accelerate student progress; life-long learning, which would provide learning tools to alumni and keep them as contributing members of the university; and distant learning, which would allow universities to share access with the greatest teachers from around the globe. Trends such as these have

76

been partially realized by universities, but their true potential has yet to be tapped.

Despite the potential, Branscomb believes that universities are still slower than businesses and the military in applying technology. He believes this has to do with lack of incentives on the part of the university, students, and faculty members, and with the lack of control universities have over their operations and faculty. Significant changes, he contends, will not take place until there are adequate incentives and until universities are willing to commit at least 10% of their total operating costs for a complete technological overhaul.

Even though faculty members are not applying the uses of technology to improving their teaching productivity, Branscomb suggests that they are making use of technology to further their own scholarly interests. He points to the number of international collaborations and amount of international traffic on Internet as evidence of this.

Branscomb also touches on a theme mentioned several times throughout this book—intellectual protectionism, or attempts to control the flows of technology across U.S. borders. American universities are expected to make significant technological contributions to national competitiveness by moving innovations to industry. This expectation leaves universities torn between their commitment to global communities and their dependence on national sources of support. For instance, by hosting foreign researchers as well as one-third of all foreign students, are they "giving away" knowledge paid for by Americans? And, by publishing "everything" in open literature, are they inadvertently favoring foreign firms who are better able to commercialize new ideas?

Branscomb concludes that universities will need to balance the two roles of making a significant contribution to the American economy and demonstrating a commitment to global knowledge. Our society, he says, must also come to the realization that its best self-interests lie in a global market of ideas and interests.

Universities are the first to create technology and the last to use it. Nevertheless, the technology they create is changing the world, and those changes are altering the character of universities and posing new challenges for their officers.

How might technology change the function and nature of universities in the future? Technological change has both direct and indirect effects on universities. The direct effects are seen in the ways technology is used by a university in the performance of its functions. Universities are the sources of many innovations in the applications of information technologies: computers, communications, video, and print, among others. But these innovations fall far short of their potential to contribute to the university's fundamental function of education. This is not a new phenomenon. Fifty-two years ago, the Association of American Colleges published a definitive study of the use of libraries in undergraduate education. It found that university libraries were vital resources for faculty research, but had very little impact on the education of undergraduates.[1] Nothing much has changed since then. Librarians have continued to push for technological modernization; the visions of 10 years ago have all been tested and many implemented.[2] But, the use of the university library has changed little. Universities are simply very conservative institutions, and the incentives to induce faculty to find innovative ways to improve instructional productivity and effectiveness are weak.

Nevertheless, digital information technology does bring a qualitatively new set of capabilities to higher education. It can be used as:

- a tool to transform how research is performed and knowledge is created and communicated
- a means for publishing, storing, and retrieving knowledge for both current and future generations
- a means for acquiring and transferring knowledge—in short, learning and teaching

The U.S. installed base of personal computers in business, government, and education (excluding homes), is expected to grow from 40 million in 1991 to 80 million in 1995.[3] Virtually every student and most faculty own and use personal computers. Although computer network usage tends to be correlated with particular academic disciplines, a great many of these computers are equipped with modems and access electronic mail.

The largest collection of interconnected networks in the world is the Internet—a collection of over 4000 networks among which electronic mail messages flow. In 1992, 107 countries were connected directly or indirectly to the Internet.[4] Anthony Rutkowsky estimates that at least 10 million people have access to the Internet worldwide, and the traffic level in 1992 was growing at over 10% per month. In the U.S., some 28 million personal computers, or 56% of all PCs installed in the U.S., will be attached to others through local area networks (LANs) by the end of 1995.[5] Many, if not most, will be attached to the Internet.

Universities had a major role in this growth. Packet switching had its origin in a project sponsored by the Advanced Research Projects Agency in the Department of Defense, but the ideas and much of the experimentation came from MIT and Bolt Beranek and Newman. The TCP-ICP protocols were developed over the years by many universities. A nationwide store-and-forward computer network called BITNET arose from an internal IBM network called "VNET," but grew rapidly in universities around the world and is now incorporated as one of the largest networks in the Internet.

University managements recognized long ago that computers represented an essential and expensive resource, and organized a consortium called Educom to pool their experience and share their capabilities. Educom became the executive agent for BITNET and today is one of the most influential organizations in defining the future of the National Research and Education Network (NREN). NREN represents a billion dollar commitment by the Congress to an upgraded, switched-broadband computer network linking universities with industrial and government laboratories.[6] Both the Bush and Clinton administrations have seen NREN as a major element of national infrastructure that is expected to contribute importantly to information diffusion.

The vision of what information technology can do for universities is appealing:

- **Computer-assisted learning.** The use of computers can increase faculty productivity and both accelerate and measure student progress. University faculties are inventing it, but few use it. Classroom lectures are still the norm. The most general use of computer-assisted learning is in the military.
- **Life-long learning.** Most universities have substantial programs in extension education; Harvard has 30,000 students studying in Harvard Extension. Some universities have cooperative programs with business employers, providing instruction over microwave and other broadband links. Others are experimenting with the provision of knowledge resources to alumni, including provision of updates to the computer programs they used as students. By providing learning tools to alumni, universities might keep alumni growing professionally and provide income to the university.
- **Distant learning.** The National Technological University has demonstrated distant learning to be a cost effective means for delivering engineering education. It provides shared access among many univer-

sities to the greatest teachers and the most distinguished scholars. But the best use of distant learning is currently being made in industry.

- **Revolution in the performance of scholarship and research.** The revolution includes collaboration with scholars around the world, access through the Internet to supercomputer centers and other shared research resources, and interactive access to mammoth stores of statistics, data, and codified knowledge of all kinds.
- **Electronic publishing.** Advances in electronic publishing are accelerating the diffusion of knowledge and lowering the cost of access. Electronic journals and new forms of shared communications, such as subject-specific "computer bulletin boards," can enhance opportunities for evaluation and criticism, create living literature through incremental enhancement of documented knowledge by qualified contributors, and aggregate a national and a world market for scholarly output.
- **Enhanced institutional effectiveness and efficiency.** Beyond providing efficiencies common to any service business, information technology can transform relationships within institutions, flattening the organization and empowering voluntary cooperative activities across organizational units while preserving the integrity of vertical lines of authority and administrative control.

All of these trends have been realized by universities to some degree. The proof is found in a painful fact: Costs of rewiring campuses, acquiring and supporting LANs, buying high-speed computers, and costs of telecommunications services are a growing and heavy burden on the scarce financial resources of universities.

Despite all the promise, the impact of technology on universities has failed to produce the transformation in their character and function that some have predicted. The limited success of some major experiments, such as the University of theWorld, organized by Professor Miller in California, seem to support this conclusion.

Why, then, are universities so much slower than business firms and the military to use technology to increase instructional productivity and effectiveness? The reasons are not mysterious:

- Universities do not pay students to learn; students pay them. In firms, the quicker the students learn, the lower the costs. Firms and the military see education as a necessary opportunity cost from their primary function. While the students are learning, they are not making money for the firm and are not available for active military service. Since most degree programs have fixed schedules for completion of requirements, tuition flows are determined by residence time, not by rates of educational progress. Thus, the incentive to the university to increase educational productivity is limited.

- For students, the incentives are not necessarily perverse. Since students pay for inputs, not outcomes, their costs are independent of how much they learn. By pressing the faculty for more productivity, their educational benefits can be enhanced at no marginal costs. Indeed, students are the most focal sources of complaints about poor teaching. But, for most of them, the task of meeting the grading hurdles set by the faculty determine their incentives to learn, enhanced perhaps by an occasional inspirational teacher. Thus, student incentives to press for more effective instruction are also limited.
- Faculties also have little incentive to increase their own teaching productivity. Their duties are typically defined by committee class hours, and their performance measured more by research distinction than by teaching effectiveness or by student learning outcomes. Since the art of measuring those outcomes is still primitive, this may be to a degree unavoidable. But, the focus of priority on research distinction may help explain why information technology is used so effectively by faculty in support of research—and in gaining recognition from their peers—but is so little used in instruction.
- Finally, universities have weak control over their own operations and faculty, and have limited resources to invest in transforming the ways they do business, even if the incentive structures were susceptible to improvement.

Against this rather pessimistic view of the incentives for use of educational technology, the technology itself continues to move ahead into new capabilities of potential value in education. Such new technologies include:

- desk-top super computers providing computing power only available from huge main-frame computers in the past
- the compact disk (CD-ROM) on which an entire encyclopedia can be stored
- multi-media computer terminals that combine text, figures, and graphics with high quality audio and video output
- the NREN, which will provide inexpensive access (per user) to an expanding resource of information services of all kinds

Until universities can command a budget equal to about 10% of their annual total operating costs for investing in educational improvement R&D and for acquiring the supporting information technology, and until universities can find ways to provide incentives to faculty and students to accept the changes that are implied in how education is accomplished, little is going to change. Where faculties do have incentives to increase their productivity in their scholarship and its external recognition, the picture is quite different. Faculties are making excellent use of information technology to further their own scholarly interests and professional careers. A study by Jean-Francois Miquel, at the Office of Technological Advancement (OTA), published in Dorothy Zinberg's The Changing University,[7] looked at international collaborations in scholarship as evidenced by multi-authored papers. In his two case studies, he found that between 1981 and 1986 scholarly collaboration in science between the U.S. and Denmark increased 22.5%, and between American and Greek authors by 97.1%. International science is apparently on the rise. The extraordinary growth of both national and international traffic on the Internet is further testimony to the number of personal relationships that transcend national borders in the academic community.

These trends will accelerate as nations turn to multi-lateral arrangements for financing scientific facilities, and as high-speed data communications allow a control room in one country to operate a research facility in another.[8] Universities may find themselves more deeply engaged in negotiations with institutions abroad (institutions that will, in many cases, not be universities but rather quasi-governmental research agencies).

Some indirect effects of technological change are having an even more profound effect on universities.

Information technology plays an important part in altering the nature of the world we live in, and hence alters expectations and opportunities for universities that are independent of the means by which universities conduct their activities. Governments are increasingly unable to control unilaterally the levels and flows of technology within and across their borders. The nature of sovereignty itself is being transformed. Universities are caught between their desire to serve their communities and their commitment to universal truth and admission open to all who qualify and can contribute.

Technology promises the university an accelerated globalization of scholarship and learning; the threat of national and regional technological competition is intellectual protectionism. My thesis is that the threat of intellectual protectionism arises from the success (and too often the excessive zeal) of universities in selling the idea that they make unique contributions to national economic performance, combined with the rapid trend to economic and intellectual globalization.

U.S. universities cannot have it both ways. In the attempt to do so, new pressures are arising and the public esteem they have enjoyed since World War II is falling.

Universities are sources of science and the seedbeds for technology. As such, they are expected to make important contributions to national competitiveness, especially in the U.S. Congress has relied heavily on legislation to encourage universities to move the knowledge they create more quickly to industry. Congress apparently does not accept that graduating well-trained students is, in fact, the fastest and most effective way to do this. Nor is Congress satisfied that the selection of research priorities by the universities matches the economic and social needs of the U.S. or of world societies.[9] The National Science Board created a Commission in September 1992 to advise it on the future of the NSF. Because of calls for NSF to couple university science more closely with U.S. industry, many academic scientists and their administrations are very nervous about the loss of academic autonomy in federally supported research.

Universities are being torn by unreasonable expectations of their role in economic performance; to a degree they have themselves to blame. They are also being torn between their commitment to global communities and their obligations as nationally chartered institutions, dependent on national sources of support. This is a special form of the economic policy issue every government must face: What criteria determine whether foreign-owned domestic firms are eligible to participate in government-funded incentives for improved economic performance? This is what Robert Reich has called the "Who's Us?" question.[10]

What charges arising from the growing importance of technological capability in international economic competition are being laid at the feet of university administrations?

- By hosting foreign researchers, especially those from foreign firms, and even by accepting endowments for professorships from foreign firms, universities are "giving away" knowledge assets paid for by American taxpayers without fair recompense.[11]
- By hosting one-third of all the foreign students in the world, U.S. universities are engaged in a massive knowledge drain.
- By publishing everything they learn in open literature, universities are favoring foreign firms that are able to commercialize new ideas more quickly than American firms. The inference is that the U.S. government should invest less in fundamental research; the alternative, of course, is for U.S. firms to accelerate their ability to acquire, adapt, and exploit new knowledge from all sources.
- By insisting on scientific autonomy and researching problems interesting to disciplinary academics rather than problems of greater interest to U.S. industry, universities are diverting scarce government resources to disciplines of low economic value.

- By working primarily within established disciplines and by strong preference for individual faculty investigator support, academics are preventing interdisciplinary research by teams of investigators who would make more rapid progress toward technologies of economic value.
- By cavalier management of indirect cost accounting and occasional lapses into scientific misconduct, universities are abrogating—or at least endangering—the social contract under which scientific autonomy was assured for the last 40 years.

My conclusion is that universities will have to walk a very delicate line between expecting recognition for the very real contribution they make to the technological roots of economic performance in this country, and the commitment to truth and scholarship without regard to national boundaries that is a prerequisite of their intellectual integrity. Striking that balance successfully is much more important, I suggest, than wiring all the buildings with optical fibers and putting a computer on every desk.

What might universities do to lessen these pressures and address the real issues? A place to start is the updating of engineering education in two directions: a) training engineers to be more astute and swifter exploiters of new science, and b) directing engineering research and education toward the acceleration of innovation and helping U.S. firms to adopt these methods. Universities should also realize that political pressures arising from concerns about U.S. competitiveness are focussing to an unreasonable degree on them. Universities should get behind a national technology strategy that addresses the waste in many, if not most, government "megaprojects," the huge allocation of government R&D funds into federal and national laboratories, where the money neither trains people for industry nor creates technology accessible and useful to industry.[12]

NOTES

1. Harvie Branscomb, *Teaching with Books* (Hamden, CT: The Shoe String Press, 1940).
2. Lewis Branscomb, "The Electronic Library," *Journal of Communication*, 31, no. 1 (Winter 1981), pp. 143-49; Lewis M. Branscomb, "The Technology of Information," in *An Information Agenda for the 1980's* (New York: New York University, 1980).
3. Dataquest's North American Market Statistics: Local Area Networks, May 1991.
4. Larry Landweber, "International Connectivity," *Internet Society News*, 1, no. 1 (January 1992), p. 3.
5. Forrester Research's Network Strategy Report: LANs for Free?, November 1991.
6. *Grand Challenges: High Performance Computing and Communications, The FY 1992 U.S. Research and Development Pattern*, a Report by the Committee on Physical,

Mathematical, and Engineering Sciences, Federal Coordinating Council for Science, Engineering, and Technology, Office of Science and Technology Policy, supplement to the President's FY 1992 Budget (Washington, DC: National Science Foundation, 1991). For a convenient summary, see U.S. Congress, Office of Technology Assessment, *High Performance Computing and Networking for Science—Background Paper*, OTA-BP-CIT-59 (Washington, DC: U.S. Government Printing Office, September 1989).

7. Dorothy S. Zinberg, ed., *The Changing University: How Increased Demand for Scientists and Technology Is Transforming Academic Institutions Internationally*, NATO ASI Series D: Behavioral and Social Sciences, Vol. 59 (Dordrecht: Kluwer Academic Publishers, 1990).

8. Because the political appeal of billion-dollar scientific facilities lies in nationalistic claims of world leadership in science and technology, it is difficult to negotiate multi-lateral support for expensive facilities and even more difficult to determine in what country they should be sited. The use of broadband communications to decentralize the location of control consoles and analysis computers for experiments opens the possibility that many countries could have the locus of key experiments within their borders, even if the central facility is elsewhere.

9. George Brown, "The Last Blank Check," *Los Angeles Times*, September 8, 1992. See also Report of the Subcommittee on Science Task Force, House Committee on Science, Space, and Technology, September 15, 1992.

10. Robert Reich, "Who's Us?" *Harvard Business Review*, (January-February 1990), p. 53.

11. This concern was raised in congressional hearings by the late Congressman Weiss of New York. More recently, legislation was introduced (and subsequently blocked) to forbid unclassified basic research funded by NSF and NIH from reaching foreign firms—an idea that is both impractical and frightening.

12. In 1990, the federal government spent $20.8 billion on R&D in the national laboratories and its own directly operated laboratories. The universities spent $20.4 billion, of which only $11.8 billion came from federal sources.

Technology and the Role of the Universities in a Global Information Economy

* * * * * * * *

Gerhard Friedrich

EXECUTIVE SUMMARY

Gerhard Friedrich asks: Will American universities be leaders or loss leaders in a knowledge-based economy? He suggests that the answer to this is up to the universities themselves. However, American universities are well positioned to play a significant role since, if the global economy is going to be knowledge-based, universities hold at least the primary raw material of that knowledge.

Friedrich discusses three types of illustrative technologies that he believes will shape the future of a knowledge-based economy. Touching on an idea introduced by Steven Muller, Friedrich believes that the network/research library will play a lead role in the area of global knowledge. The problem, he contends, will be determining whose protocols and standards will become the norm. Broadband satellite tele-communication will provide the opportunity for individuals in different parts of the world to meet via a computer confer-ence. Another example of an illustrative technology that could have a tremendous impact on higher education is global imaging. Friedrich points to a University of California project, Sequoia 2000, that stores massive amounts of environmental data about the earth and visually displays this information in real time. Friedrich suggests that such a concept might allow higher education institutions to model knowledge flows.

Friedrich questions whether higher education will have a role to play in the molding and shaping of these technologies and suggests possible scenarios. The Community of Learning Information Network, funded by the U.S. Chamber of Commerce, is hoping to link schools and libraries in over 100 communities around the country via a satellite link-up. Under this scenario, school buildings could be used after hours by small businesses for training employees and by the military for training their personnel. Universities could participate in a number of ways, such as providing educational materials. On a more global level, Friedrich speaks of a scenario that merges business/administrative systems with personal systems and knowledge systems in a triangle, with the entire knowledge processing capability in the middle. Higher education needs to determine which kind of role it could play in these kinds of scenarios.

Finally, Friedrich suggests that increased advances in technology may radically change the definition of a "classroom," and challenge the need for a traditional campus.

When I was first asked to talk about technology in the global university, a title immediately came to mind. Is the university going to be a leader or a loss leader in the global knowledge-based economy? My objective is to be provocative and to suggest that, if the global economy is in fact going to be knowledge-based, then the university holds at least the primary raw material of that knowledge. There's a critical choice at this point that has finance as well as leadership implications: will the university play the knowledge/economy equivalent of an industrial strip mine, or a more active role as the refiner of raw materials? I will approach the question by describing several leading edge technology examples involving universities and provide some likely scenarios. I will conclude with my notions about the role that the university needs to play, and some short-term decisions that I believe will challenge core values of the university and provide opportunities for leadership. My goal is not necessarily to be comprehensive, either in describing technology or global geo-political trends.

Let me begin by discussing illustrative technologies. The network/research library is now a point of great innovation. Years ago, who would have thought that librarians would come to be the innovative leaders in the adoption of technology? They have moved our institutions towards an almost ubiquitous use of global networks. The problem, however, is connecting very different and very deeply grounded institutions. The next stage of growth will need to deal with that problem. I believe the issue (as with all "religious" wars) is coming to a temporary truce, and determining whose standards and which international protocols and formats will prevail over the next decade. What we will see in the next five years is the transmission of large amounts of con-textual-based retrieval. A new capacity will emerge to retrieve and make sense out of the information that is being put on these networks by research librar-ies. Incidentally, research libraries are now being joined by museums and art galleries as we move into much broader and richer multi-media capabilities; digitally, we can now store virtual moving images of dinosaurs, as well as fairly pure replications of art masterpieces. These ubiquitous networks allow us to store, transmit, and access the thesaural as well as the bibliographical; various conceptual and contextual-based retrieval systems allow all of that to be stored and retrieved around the world.

Data were raw material prior to the information economy. Certainly infor-mation, which has begun to be broadly distributed in financial institutions, has led us to see the value of an information-based economy. The question now is which institutions will be the first to see the value of a knowledge-based economy? Global banks and financial institutions took the leadership in the information economy. Who will take the leadership role in the knowl-edge-based economy? I think that the multi-media aspect is going to be avail-able within the next five to eight years, much quicker than we would have predicted. In fact, I would go further and say that both the transmission issue and the translation issue across languages will be solved. Out of the linguistic breakthroughs and linguistic and context-based retrieval, we will be able to make a significant dent in meaning translation as well as word and lexicon translation. I predict that the transmission, transformation, and translation of information to more usable knowledge in scholarly pursuits will be ubiqui-tous by the end of the twentieth century.

Another illustrative possibility is broadband satellite telecommunication. One example, from the University of Arizona, is a fascinating initiative called the "mirror project," which takes telecommunications and video conferencing to the next level. It allows you to enter a conference room where there is a circular table and three large screens on which you can watch other people in Tokyo, London, or Paris enter their similarly arranged conference rooms. Since the screen is large, it gives you the virtual reality; it looks like everyone is actually sitting at one large table. This technology allows a classroom or a meeting of college and university presidents to include participants from around the world. Researchers who once communicated via computer conferencing and through research/publishing exchanges can now sit down together in a virtual classroom for "face-to-face" interaction. Taking this capability to its logical conclusion, and given the fact that costs for this kind of broadband satellite communication are falling drastically, the notion of location-dependent education in international study takes on a different meaning.

Another example involves global imaging and a University of California project called Sequoia 2000, the first part of a NASA program called the Earth Observation System. This system allows disparate and interdisciplinary researchers to access massive amounts of data and visual imagery about global warming and about economic and environmental trends from around the globe. The researchers are able to enter that data in a massively parallel processing super computer center, and store it on over 150,000 video and storage disks. This allows them to dynamically model and visually display a changing pattern of the earth's atmosphere in real time, providing dramatic visual impact. I chose this example because massive parallel processing, super computing, and global imaging systems have key roles to play in the future. It is not that far-fetched to think that we could begin to look at similar models that dynamically update the world economic picture, or the world political picture. It is also not inconceivable to use systems of this sort and the conceptual model not only to examine the world financial transaction movement, but to model something as elusive as the world balance of knowledge trade. At this point, I have few clues about how to build such a system. However, when we look at the Sequoia Project and see interdisciplinary researchers sharing their data and beginning to develop common pictures and ways of understanding and modeling the world, we can see the possibility of educators discussing the modeling of knowledge flows. Universities hold, shape, and mold these technologies constantly.

The molding and shaping of those technologies raises a fundamental question: Will universities be able to play a role in capitalizing as a player in the world economy? What is very clear now is that we now have the capability to build the infrastructure. I would like to offer one quick scenario that is not entirely far-fetched, and not quite on the global imaging scale. This one comes from the U.S. Chamber of Commerce. It concerns grades K-12, but it also has implications for higher education. The U.S. Chamber of Commerce has been funding a private institution called the Community of Learning and Information Network, which involves the U.S. departments of Education, Labor, and Defense. As peace has broken out and more of our military forces are put on reserve status, maintaining the national readiness of our troops is a primary concern. Since reservists live in every community in the country, why not make use of the resources available in every community, such as schools and libraries, to help maintain that readiness. The Community Learning Network is proposing that the military invest in the infrastructure by installing a satellite down-link system that would connect over 100 communities around the country. The plan would allow the school building to be used from 8:00 am to 4:00 pm for K-12 instruction. Small businesses would be given access from 4:00 pm to 8:00 pm for employee continuing education, since they can't afford investments in corporate education the way the large firms do. Then from 8:00 pm to midnight, the military could use the building for training. This concept has great political appeal. It addresses education reform, stimulates growth in the economy, and capitalizes on the peace dividend, all in one stroke. The investment to implement that satellite technology is almost a rounding error in the military budget. And, instantly, the infrastructure for changing the nature of how education gets developed, distributed, and market-driven, across the United States at least, begins to open up, just as the military has provided infrastructure in roads and bridges in the past. One way that universities can participate economically is by providing educational material over that distribution network. They can play a pivotal role in shaping the community and corporate educational picture. This is a likely scenario, but I leave it to you to determine whether it will happen.

Let me move from that local scenario to a more global one. Dr. Juan Rada, a former director general of IMD in Switzerland, has an interesting model of how the global information technology industry is changing in structure and form in it's next generation. He has a triangulated view of how business and administrative systems are beginning to merge with the traditional personal computer systems. Personal systems in his mind, and in the minds of others, include the advent of HDTV; and computer notebooks, satellite uplinks, and students being able to walk around campus taking notes on flora and fauna. The third leg of that global industry stool is what he would call knowledge systems. The participants in knowledge systems at the moment are not only the publishers and the broadcasters, the universities and educators, but also the entertainment industry. Rada projects not only a convergence of the players in those industries but opportunities for a great deal of strategic alliance and business across each one of those legs. At the center of that triangle is the entire knowledge processing capability. The question that we all have is what role will universities and educators have in pulling this together? Strange bedfellows will come out of these new alliances, and I hesitate to use the word alliances because I think a lot of strategic alliances in the 1980s ran into all sorts of difficulties, both legally and economically. The analogy that one could apply is that these will be schools of fish that will learn to swim together. The fish with different specializations will help guide the total industry through various shoals depending on the specialty that is most appropriate at the time that new product introduction or materials/technology introduction occurs. It is not unlikely, for example, that the University of Florida, in conjunction with Walt Disney World, would want to develop a new global education corporation or enterprise. They could look to Reuters and AT&T and IBM to swim in their school as they introduce a new global education corporation called "EducationWorld," instead of Walt Disney World. And maybe Harvard, the Smithsonian, George Lucas, Ted Turner, CNN, and the global communications and technology companies of their choice could get together and add new meaning to a company called "Star Search." What we would see are lots of reasons why education corporations will have more private players, and why the university should be one of those players.

Another example worth noting is the growing reputation of the consortium known as the National Technical University (NTU). MIT certainly is participating in it, and total participation now numbers in the fifties. NTU catalogs now have to be carried around in wheelbarrows. The phenomenon of being a "campusless" university, of involving the best educators, and allowing students to learn from anywhere in the world is not something that I would want to overlook. The time and space issues, and the "campuslessness" issue of being able to distribute incidentally through video conferencing, will begin to challenge the need for traditional campuses in the not-too-near future. The time element of assuming that degrees have to be completed in two- or four-year increments, versus the problem of front loading a four-year education onto a constantly changing career or research pattern, certainly ought to bring up a reexamination of the notion of career-long education and the cooperative nature of education. And education could be driven as much by the speed to learn as it is by the speed to educate. And I would also say that notions of academic freedom versus charging for access to information, are putting rather large cracks into traditional methods of learning.

In conclusion, I think the short-term role of universities will be to continue to have and to stimulate more interdisciplinary discussions and programs. You have within the university the knowledge and interdisciplinary skills to address the economic, technological, political policy, and behavioral science issues. Can U.S. universities refocus change in the face of this kind of discontinuity, embrace the issue of risk, learn business affiliation skills and competition, and lead and innovate in time to be entrepreneurial players in the economy, rather than exploited partners? This economy does not allow for observers and commentators. Universities are best positioned as players and coaches. How well universities begin to play that role is the thought I leave you with.

Planning for Internationalization: Experience at the University of Pennsylvania

* * * * * * * * *

Michael Aiken

EXECUTIVE SUMMARY

Michael Aiken discusses Penn's five-year plan to further the university's international activities. Goals were set not only for the university as a whole (for instance, raising from 20% to 40% the number of students who study abroad), but all the deans were asked to prepare five-year plans within their respective departments. The plan has the full support of the University's Board of Trustees; they created a permanent committee on internationalization in 1992, which will receive formal status reports on the University's progress at least three times a year. Formed only 18 months ago, the program is still too new to evaluate. However, Aiken believes that there are eight issues involved with the plan that are worthy of discussion.

One of the primary issues facing the program is under-graduate foreign students and financial aid. Should financial aid monies be used for foreign students at the undergraduate

92

level? The central question, Aiken suggests, is does being an international university mean educating foreign students or does it mean making domestic students more internationally competent? Other issues Aiken discusses include: encouraging faculty to teach nontraditional languages, maintaining quality for those students who study in overseas institutions and the enclave vs. immersion issue, internationalizing the curriculum by possibly creating minors in international studies, and bringing more international experiences to campus for those students who will not have the opportunity to go overseas. Finally, Aiken discusses Penn's plan for overseas development—reaching the many alumni who live overseas and, because of their culture, may not be geared towards a "philanthropic orientation."

The University of Pennsylvania has been working hard to make internationalization a reality on campus. I will give a progress report of our activities, raise several issues and questions, and share some of the problems that we have faced during this process. We used several kinds of administrative mechanisms to further internationalization at Penn. We put together a five-year plan, which was published about 18 months ago, and we are establishing benchmarks to see what has been accomplished. We created a council with a delegate from each of our 12 schools that coordinates all the international programs. All deans were asked to take the elements within that five-year plan and establish five-year plans within their schools. The Board of Trustees was given a presentation about our efforts to internationalize. They were so interested in this issue that they immediately set up an ad hoc committee on internationalization and created a permanent committee this past June. Three times a year, progress reports will go to this committee, and a three-year implementation plan is being prepared to fulfill some of our goals. I would like to share eight elements of the program and discuss some of the dilemmas and problems the program faces.

The first issue is *foreign students on campus,* who make up about 9% of Penn's undergraduates and 25% of graduate students. In 1980, 13 years ago, only 2% of our undergraduate students were foreign. Since then, we have had a deliberate policy of bringing more undergraduate students to our campus. Very little of our financial aid money has been allocated for foreign students at the undergraduate level; there are no restrictions at the graduate level. What this means is that, at 9%, we have reached the limit on the number of foreign undergraduate students we can enroll, unless we do something about financial aid. We are wrestling with a very big problem, both with our trustees and our faculty, over the question "What does it mean to be an international university?" Does it mean educating students from around the world? Or does it mean educating domestic students with "international competence?" A big question facing Penn and many universities is the use of financial aid monies for international students at the undergraduate level.

Foreign language is a second key element. Many of us can identify with Professor Lester Thurow's comments about the frustrations associated with trying to get faculty from traditional language departments to teach language courses other than such popular ones as French and Spanish. We have addressed this at our university by creating a new structure, the Penn Language Center, part of our College of General Studies. The Center offers courses for less frequently taught languages, such as Korean and business Korean. While we teach Japanese in the department, we teach business Japanese at the Center.

Faculty exchange is another potential problem. It is easy to go around the world and make agreements; it is not so easy to involve faculty in these kinds of things if they are not already involved. This is an area where we have experienced many problems, such as the constraints of dealing with currency and exchanges in the new nations of the former USSR. On the other hand, my experience has shown this to be an ideal time for American universities to approach Europe because European administrators are having to make administrative adjustments to accommodate both student and faculty exchanges.

A fourth element that we have focused on is *study abroad*. Currently, about 20% of Penn students go overseas—for a summer, a semester, or a year. Our goal is to raise that to 40% over the next five years. Of the many problems that come to fore in this area, one of the primary ones is quality. How do you maintain quality for programs and for students? Many of us charge high tuitions and, as a result, students have certain expectations with regard to their educational programs. There is a major dilemma in trying to create programs in countries such as France, Italy, or Spain, because most of the universities there have between 100,000 and 150,000 students, with as many as 300 students in a lecture session. This poses a problem for students who are paying $18,000 a year. Making the arrangements for study abroad is not the issue— the issue is running quality programs. Another problem in the area of study abroad is the question of total immersion vs. an enclave. We find ourselves creating enclaves to protect our students, while at the same time wanting to immerse them in the culture they are visiting. We set up a program in Korea where we were able to obtain the best of both worlds. With our program, the students have an English language program, which is basically an enclave. And, if their performance in the language course is good enough, the students can go into the other courses. As Professor Lyman mentioned in the

Introduction, very few students in the United States have the capacity to deal with languages of the Far East, such as Korean or Chinese, at least not at the undergraduate level. The problem is that if they did not take the language at the undergraduate level, they probably would not take it at the graduate level.

A fifth area that we tried to work on is *graduate and professional student exchanges*. This is an area where we've had the most success. These types of exchanges will proceed primarily by the facilitation of faculty exchanges, because the graduate students will tend to follow their faculty members. I see a possible dilemma in that many of us are trying to reduce the time required to obtain a Ph.D. in our graduate programs. If we begin to send students abroad in the early stages of their Ph.D. program, it seems to me that it would be counterproductive. Consequently, we have to think about the fields and about tailoring to the best time in the Ph.D. program when the students can profit from these kinds of experiences.

Another element that we try to work on is *area programs*. Professor Lyman touches upon the tension between the area specialist and the disciplinary specialist. My field of sociology is not producing area specialists. Political science is probably doing less well in this regard today than it was 20 years ago. So, in this area, we are losing ground, not just at Penn, but at other institutions as well. The generation trained in the 1960s is about ready to retire and we do not have sufficient replacements. This whole issue of revitalizing our area programs is a very serious one, because the people with the specialties are not out there. I think the problem of finding internal sources and creating horizontal mechanisms that can support these sources is much easier to solve than the issue of personnel in this area.

A seventh area, perhaps the biggest challenge of all, is how we *internationalize the curriculum* and how we get our faculty to build an international content. I am hopeful that my deans are going to tell me how they're going to do this when they give us their five-year plans. Some of the approaches we are considering include creating minors in international studies for undergraduates, thereby creating a captive market for those students in area programs. Curricular development grants are familiar to all of us, but we have had limited experience of whether they stick or not. Internationalizing the curriculum is one of the biggest challenges I see. The Wharton School is actively trying to internationalize, but it faces the same problem of finding faculty with international experience and knowledge to build into its program.

The eighth part of our program is the *simulation of international experiences*. Not all of our students are going to go overseas; how can we provide the same kind of sensitivity to other cultures? One of the great advantages I see of internationalism is that you can address the problems that are posed by the politically correct multiculturalism argument and place them in a different framework. One reason for pursuing internationalism is that it takes away from some of the domestic implications of multiculturalism. We tried through learning arrangements in our dormitories where, for instance, we set aside floors so students can opt to live in an environment where only Chinese or Japanese was spoken. We also tried to support our nationality clubs. The question that has been raised: "Are we supporting ghettoization?" or "Are we supporting all these language groups and cultural groups that will be open to undergraduates?" I would like to think the latter; I'm fearful of the former.

These are the kinds of things we are trying to do in our academic programs. I think another whole issue of internationalization is to turn our attention towards development and our alumni overseas. We have done a very self-conscious evaluation of where our money comes from overseas. Our business school does a superb job in this regard, but we have many alumni that we have not yet tapped. I think another whole issue of internationalization is to turn our attention towards development overseas. What I have learned over the last couple of years is that this is not a short-term program in development. Even though the people that we are working with may be alumni, cultural factors are going to make our efforts extremely slow in terms of getting payoffs. At the same time, however, I think we have to do it. As part of our planning, we are going to send the president, the provost, and all the deans on the road frequently, so that we have a presence. Foundations and corporations overseas are somewhat helpful. However, as we have already heard, it is not in the culture of most European or Eastern countries to have a philanthropic orientation. There has to be some sort of cultural change before we can be really successful.

"Internationalizing" the Liberal Arts College

❖ ❖ ❖ ❖ ❖ ❖ ❖ ❖

Stephen R. Lewis, Jr.

EXECUTIVE SUMMARY

Stephen Lewis outlines what he believes is necessary to internationalize an institution, particularly the liberal arts college, and the conditions under which this internationalizing process can be nurtured. He focuses on the history and success of the "International 50," a group of liberal arts colleges with a great degree of international "reach" that was convened in 1991. Even though, as a group, these 50 institutions account for only 1.8% of all baccalaureate degrees granted in this country, they represent a disproportionate percentage of American higher education's involvement in international activities. For instance, graduates of the International 50 represent 20% of all American students who received Ph.D.s in Japanese. Of the 50 institutions, 30 also participate in "The Oberlin Group," a set of 50 science-specialized institutions. Lewis believes that the International 50's success in both international education and science specialization is worth examining.

Using the International 50 and Carleton College as models, Lewis offers several conditions under which he believes internationalization on a campus may flourish. Included among them are the hiring of faculty who both fill departmental needs and have an interest in international affairs, increased faculty support for study abroad programs and recognition of those faculty members who do so, more

*respect for language teaching, integration of international
activities with on-campus activities, and increased portability of scholarships. Most important, the college must have
senior administrators and faculty who are staunch supporters
of international activity.*

As is generally true among American colleges and universities, liberal
arts colleges are primarily in the *sending* rather than the *receiving* business in the international student exchange. And, as is also generally
true, U.S. undergraduates tend to go abroad for a relatively small portion of
their educational experience, while international students coming to the
United States tend to be here for a degree program, whether at the graduate
or the undergraduate institution.

My remarks will be addressed to the undergraduate, principally at liberal
arts colleges. I will discuss a group calling itself "the International 50," and I
will talk about Carleton College. I will try to indicate what I believe constitutes "internationalizing" an institution and the conditions that nurture it.
These thoughts are based on experience both at Carleton and at Williams
College, where I taught for 21 years, as well as observation of other institutions, including two in the "International 50."

The International 50 liberal arts colleges were originally convened in 1991
under that auspices of Beloit College inWisconsin. The group was chosen
inductively, looking at the evidence about international participation of students, faculty, and alumni of various institutions with the greatest degree of
international "reach" among the category of liberal arts institutions as classified by the Carnegie Commission.

While these 50 institutions generate roughly 1.8% of all baccalaureate
degrees granted in the United States, they are disproportionately more involved in international ventures, and disproportionately contribute to the
various forms of "outcomes" that may be important to American society. At
the extreme, for example, the graduates of the International 50 constituted
20% of all those who received Ph.D.s in Japanese and 15% of all those who
received Ph.D.s in Russian nationally, despite their relatively small contribution to total baccalaureate production.

Among the disproportionate representation in international outputs or
incomes, expressed as a ratio of the International 50 to other institutions, are
the following:

11:1	Ph.D.s in Japanese
8.5:1	Ph.D.s in Russian

6.5:1	Ph.D.s in European History
6:1	U.S. ambassadors
6:1	Enrolled in graduate schools of international affairs
5:1	Majored in foreign language or area studies
5:1	U.S. foreign service officers
5:1	Ph.D.s in any international field
4:1	Lawyers specializing in international law
4:1	Studied a foreign language at undergraduate level
4:1	Studied abroad
2.5:1	Joined the Peace Corps

In general, the graduates of the International 50 were not only high in international inputs and outcomes relative to the overall population of baccalaureate degree winners in the United States, but also high relative to their peers who graduated from undergraduate divisions of the research universities. And, with respect to study abroad, the International 50 students tended to be more highly concentrated in Asia, Africa, Latin America, the Caribbean, and the countries of the former Soviet Union and Eastern Europe than were their counterparts at other institutions.

Carleton College is at the high end of the distribution for these international participation rates. For example, about two-thirds of our students now study abroad before they graduate. And, among Carleton students who have studied abroad recently, more than 40% have studied *outside* Europe, as compared with less than a quarter nationally. Participation by men and women is almost the same as their representation in our student body, while nationally, the ratio of women to men is roughly 2 to 1 in study abroad. And, while science majors tend to be disproportionately *under-represented* nationally in study abroad programs, in recent years more than half of Carleton's biology and geology majors studied abroad. The Chemistry Department at Carleton has recently reviewed its schedule of courses to see if undertaking a study abroad program can be made more convenient for chemistry majors.

Along with international education, the International 50 also do well in science specializations. Indeed, 30 of the International 50 were also included in the 50 science-specialized institutions sometimes known as "The Oberlin Group." In a sense, these institutions "going against the grain" in two areas of national importance. How is this being accomplished?

The International 50 includes 22 institutions from "the heartland" of the United States, including 14 in either the Associated Colleges of the Midwest or the Great Lakes Colleges Association—both associations established to facilitate and share the costs and staffing of programs abroad. While the International 50 includes many of the "usual suspects" in lists of liberal arts colleges, it also includes such less well-known participants as Principia College and Goshen College, institutions chosen for inclusion in the group by objective criteria relating to their disproportionate representation in international "outcomes." Their selection was also probably due, as in the case of some of the Quaker colleges, to the long traditions and international connections of those church-related institutions.

The national interest in these outputs should be very clear. A lack of U.S. language competence among a broad base of the population and a lack of U.S. knowledge of other cultures of importance to the United States are serious and growing concerns. The end of the Cold War and the revival of "old nationalisms" have made an understanding of differences in language, culture, history, and religion increasingly important. This is true both in doing business and in understanding and taking an active role in foreign policy. For example, on a recent visit to Carleton, the Japanese ambassador to the United States noted that while there were 35,000 Japanese studying in the United States, there were less than 2,000 Americans studying in Japan. The willingness of the nationals of other countries to take the time and make the effort to understand the language and culture of their world trading partners should give pause to the United States. In an article some years ago in one of the weekly news magazines on the importance of language learning internationally, a Japanese businessman was asked, "What is the most important language in the world?" The businessman smiled and said, quietly, "My customer's." We should take note.

It is also important nationally that the country maintain a "capital goods industry" in foreign languages and in foreign history and culture if these subjects are to be taught in the future. Therefore, there must be a continuing flow of individuals with the competencies to provide instruction in these areas at the college and university levels, as well as at the elementary and secondary levels.

National interests are important, but an international perspective, a fundamentally different perspective, is also an important and genuine part of a liberal arts education. Learning about one's self and being reflective about one's own experience and beliefs—fundamental aspects of liberal learning—are functions that are greatly aided by being in and learning from another culture. Therefore, programs that provide fundamentally different perspectives on campus, as well as an off-campus experience in another culture or country, are important aspects of liberal learning.

Liberal arts colleges enjoy an enormous luxury in putting together international programs, they can internationalize both their curriculum and the experience of their undergraduates. A former colleague of mine, Dudley Bahlman, used to say as he gave his talk on the curriculum, "The best curriculum is the one that interferes least with a student's education." The liberal arts colleges are in a much better position to defy what President Emeritus Richard Lyman has called "the iron law of specialization" and to embrace Ernie Boyer's urge that we broaden the definition of hardship. The undergraduate institutions do not have to face the demands of field specialties and sub-specialties that are imposed on graduate institutions (and, generally, on their undergraduate divisions as well). We must encourage breadth and synthesis in scholarship and in teaching among our faculty.

Since Carleton has a relatively large international participation, however measured, among students and faculty, let me speculate a bit on what I believe to be the conditions under which a real internationalization of campus, curriculum, and student experience may flourish.

1. In most institutions, departments are the locus of faculty appointments. Appointments of individuals who fill real departmental or disciplinary needs but who also have a geographic area specialty or interest in international affairs are needed. Such appointments will generally require the support of deans and presidents and appointment committees from the faculty as a whole.

2. On the issue of appointments, it is important to recognize that, at the *undergraduate* level, the discipline (economics, political science, history, sociology, anthropology, religion) can be taught by studying a variety of substantive topics or areas. This means that, in general, there is little, if any, conflict between strong disciplinary programs and strength in international areas, *provided* the appointments are made well.

3. Faculty, and senior administrators, must have a broad sense of ownership of the approach to internationalize both the curriculum and student experiences. This will generally mean a faculty committee that has a fair amount of oversight over any college-sponsored off-campus studies programs or over the approval of programs taken at other institutions (U.S.-sponsored or foreign).

4. As a part of this ownership, faculty must support the programs enough to help students with scheduling issues, particularly those related to study abroad. This means such things as examining sequential requirements in science departments to make sure there are possible options to take a quarter or a semester off campus.

5. Language teaching must be both respected and linked to other aspects of area studies. The former is really a matter both for the language faculties and the general "culture" of the campus. The latter is everybody's job. Programs in French Studies, Russian Studies, East Asian Studies, etc. can both enrich the teaching of language and reinforce the objectives of area studies programs.

6. Both study abroad and teaching abroad need encouragement and support. Some form of off-campus or international studies office to facilitate the movement of both study and teaching off campus is

extremely important. The faculty who go abroad and who have international interests will invigorate the curriculum both for those who have studied abroad and for those who have not. Carleton has a very high share of students studying abroad; over 60% of those students do so on a *Carleton-sponsored* program, and another 15% or more study on Carleton-related programs of the Associated Colleges of the Midwest, Associated Kyoto Program, etc., where Carleton faculty teach either regularly or occasionally.

7. Points 5 and 6 help ensure an integration of study abroad with what happens on campus, both in the language departments and in other departments. Interestingly, such integration generates an interest among students in the professional activities of the faculty, which helps support the international focus of faculty teaching in regular line departments. Not incidentally, this integration of one's own faculty and students in study abroad also helps create a *student* demand for language teaching, so it becomes seen somewhat less as a requirement imposed from above and more as a response to student interest and need.

8. Money is important. We have found that scholarship portability is a critical element in making sure that our participation in study abroad is as high as it is. In Carleton-sponsored programs, we try to minimize the added cost of an overseas experience and look at the combined study abroad programs as well as the budgets for each individual program in assessing the financial viability. Since normally less than 10% of our student body is away in any given term, we are able to treat each foreign program as one that needs only to cover its marginal costs, which is an important element of assuring financial viability.

9. Money is also important for faculty development in these areas. A specialty in the art of China or the history of southern India is just as likely to require added faculty development costs as a speciality in solid state physics or organic chemistry. Deans, presidents, and faculty development committees need to recognize that fact.

10. "Venture capital" is also needed to help faculty explore a possibility of new programs in new geographic areas. This can clearly be linked to money for faculty development purposes for individual faculty; and, the participation of faculty members in study abroad programs can be linked to their own opportunities for faculty development. At Carleton, faculty members frequently have taken a study abroad program and then stayed on for a term of sabbatical leave in the same region. This extends their period of time in the region as well as meeting some of the costs of getting there and back on an education program.

11. It is also important for deans, presidents, and departments to give appropriate "credit" or recognition of faculty effort and expertise for purposes of tenure, salary review, and promotion, in relation to faculty activities in promoting and carrying out international programs on campus and programs abroad for students.

12. It is also important that the institution be explicit in recognizing the value of interdisciplinary or geographically oriented or international scholarship by its faculty. Similarly, it is important that participation in area studies be explicitly valued in faculty reviews. In recent years, we at Carleton have found it helpful to include in a departmental review committee for an individual being evaluated for tenure a person from the interdisciplinary program in which a faculty member has a significant amount of teaching responsibility.

13. In general, we must all recognize there are *many* complementaries— for faculty, for scholarship, for student experiences, for study abroad programs, for "internationalizing the curriculum," for interdisciplinary work in general, and for the demand for languages on the part of students. We must also recognize that each activity provides a great deal of "synergy" for the outputs of other parts of the equation.

I believe that the colleges that are successful in internationalizing their curriculum, their faculty, and the experience of their students have some mixture of the various aspects listed above. Perhaps most importantly, they tend to have presidents, deans, and a number of highly respected and high-profile faculty who are active participants in and promoters of the international effort. Finally, I think it is no accident that these same colleges appear regularly in the lists of those whose faculties are unusually productive in terms of scholarship and whose students go on in disproportionate numbers to positions of responsibility in American society.

Responding to International Challenges at MIT

* * * * * * * *

Charles Vest

EXECUTIVE SUMMARY

Can American universities, particularly research universities, serve the economic interests of this country and, at the same time, maintain a free exchange of ideas, people, and resources worldwide? According to Charles Vest, a study group at MIT addressed this question and concluded that universities can not only serve both roles, but that maintaining a preeminence in science and engineering research is one of the best ways universities can serve the vital economic interests of this country. Over the past several years, there has been a major change in which types of institutions would be key players in the international community. While the scientific and research communities are known to have been the prototypes for international cooperation, Vest points out that research universities are increasingly taking on that role. This change has been due to the increased economic value associated with the types of knowledge and technological concepts generated by American universities. Vest discusses four types of international interactions currently taking place at MIT.

Research interactions *are a significant part of MIT's international experiences, and approximately 3% of MIT's campus research is foreign-sponsored. Vest discusses the licensing of MIT inventions, which must adhere to a substantial domestic manufacturing provision, as well as three conditions that must be met by all of MIT's research programs.* The Industrial Liaison Program *(ILP) builds relationships between MIT and the industrial world by helping the university keep abreast of the research of member companies; nearly half of the 235 corporations that participate in the ILP are located overseas.* Faculty contact *with corporations around the world is another type of international interaction, with consulting being the primary activity.* Vest *points out that nearly one-third of faculty surveyed from MIT's Science, Engineering, and Management schools said they had passed on information to U.S. industries that resulted from foreign-sponsored research. A final type of international interaction described by Vest is the* MIT-Japan Program, *where participating MIT freshmen and sophomores are immersed in courses dealing with Japanese language, culture, and business practices, while still on the MIT campus; following graduation, these students study as interns in Japan.*

Universities throughout the country are currently thinking very hard about both their national and international roles and how these roles interact. This subject for introspection falls into two categories. First, in view of the growing opportunities and responsibilities in this highly interdependent and increasingly accessible world, how do we educate students to work in the global marketplace? Second, and just as important, how do we develop strong continuing intellectual ties with the rest of the world?

The second set of issues tends to pit national economic interests against worldwide development of science and technology. Both our opportunities and our responsibilities in these more problematic areas of international relations are particularly difficult in a time of considerable economic stress.

Just a few years ago most observers would have found some of the debates in which we are now engaged simply unthinkable. I believe that the nation viewed itself as generous, and that universities prided themselves on their international stature and interactions. Indeed, we pointed with pride to the cosmopolitan nature of our campuses, to the richness that our international students brought to us, and to the importance of leaders around the world

having experienced American education and student life and having connected with us during their formative years. The scientific and research community has always prided itself on being the prototype for true international
cooperation.

Today this viewpoint and system are being challenged—primarily because
of the increasing economic value of university-generated knowledge and technological concepts. I think virtually everyone would agree that truly fundamental scientific knowledge, insofar as it continues to exist, should be the
common property of all people.

Many would say, however, that the treatment of technological knowledge,
techniques, and methodologies is quite different. Advances in these areas are
more likely to have immediate economic value and, thus, take on a proprietary nature and become ensnared in matters of patents, export controls, and
so forth. This matter is complicated by the fact that the boundary between
fundamental scientific knowledge and what is considered to be technological
in nature and economically important is becoming increasingly blurred. In
any event, applied scientific and technological knowledge are generated in
many nations and, I believe, international discourse is as important to researchers in those fields as to truly fundamental science. Clearly, this opens
the door to debate about the national versus the international roles and responsibilities of universities.

The issue is complex and we are not honest with ourselves if we do not
admit that at the start. Clearly, we must be concerned with our nation's economic well-being. Our research universities are national institutions; they
are bred from a partnership between government and academia that goes
back largely to the days following World War II. These universities have served
as seedbeds for the creation and improvement of American industry. Funded
to a significant extent by the American taxpayer, they are dedicated to the
education of many of the most talented youth of our country. Therefore, the
key question, in my view, is how can we continue to serve America well,
while still maintaining the free exchanges of ideas, people, and resources that
are essential to the advancement of knowledge and to the enhancement of
life for people all across the globe?

A few years ago, we posed this question of how to succeed in this delicate
balancing act to a study group of MIT faculty, chaired by Professor Gene
Skolnikoff. In a report issued in May 1992, the committee concluded that
MIT, while international in stature and population, is "A national institution
rooted in American culture and traditions and an integral part of the nation's
education and research system." As such, it has a special obligation to serve
the interests of this country. But, and this is really the key point in the way we
have thought about this matter at MIT, the committee noted that we will
serve this country best by maintaining a pre-eminence in science and engi-

neering education, and in research that requires a strong set of ties through-out the world.

In short, even if our more narrow focus is to serve America well, we must participate in a meaningful way in the broad, global community. With this background in mind, I'd like to sketch out roughly four kinds of interactions, drawn from MIT's experience, in the hope that they may stimulate further discussion.

First, we have international *research interactions*, including interactions with foreign corporations. At MIT, about 15% of our research volume comes from industry. About 20% of that comes from foreign-based companies; in other words, about 3% of our campus research is foreign-sponsored. There are many people out there who, for a variety of reasons, simply do not like the idea of information flowing outward across our boundaries, nor research support flow-ing in, and they often suspect that patent licenses associated with such sup-port are a significant source of overseas technology transfer. What are the facts at MIT? Currently, all licensees of MIT inventions, regardless of their sponsorship, must agree to a substantial domestic manufacturing provision. This provision is modeled on, but is thougher than, the federal regulation which stipulates that, with regard to federally sponsored inventions, "a sub-stantial amount of domestic manufacturing must take place" if any of the products are going to be sold in this country. We apply this provision to ev-erything, regardless of the source of funding that may have been behind the invention. MIT issues a little over 100 U.S. patents each year. That is close to 20% of all the patents licensed by U.S. universities for the past three years. In fiscal year 1990, which is the last period for which I have a full set of data, 84% of all these licenses were with U.S. firms and 16% were with foreign firms that have U.S. facilities. In light of these figures, I think it is difficult to argue that technology is being transferred in any untoward way across the seas, at least through the granting of licenses.

Our basic belief is that our research programs are appropriately reflective of our academic and national responsibilities as long as we meet three condi-tions. The first is that, regardless of who sponsors the program, whether it's our own government or a foreign corporation, any MIT faculty member who is outside of that program is free to pursue his or her research, even if the subject is similar to or in competition with that of a sponsored program. Sec-ond, all of the resulting research must have the same conditions of access as any other research at the Institute and will be reported freely and openly. The only real exception to that is not on campus but through the Lincoln Labora-tory. Any campus research, regardless of its source, must meet the same funda-mental conditions. And finally, and this is very important given the politics of the world today, there are no restrictions, other than academic, placed on the kinds of students who can take part in research. So, for example, we would not accept sponsored research from "Country A" if there were conditions that stipulated that only a student with a specific ethnic background or from "Country B" could participate.

We have another kind of interaction with foreign corporations that is criticized from time to time. Our Industrial Liaison Program (ILP), which has been in existence for decades at MIT, is designed to build mutually beneficial relationships between MIT and the industrial world. Many other universities have a similar program in one form or another, although rarely as extensive or as centrally organized as MIT's.

Each ILP member company pays an annual fee to become a member of the program, and is assigned a staff member, called an industrial liaison officer. That officer works with each company to help us stay abreast of the company's research and business priorities and to help structure our interactions with the company. One of the things that we do when we work with ILP companies is to educate ourselves about their goals, priorities, and interests. We facilitate meetings between our faculty and their staff, sponsor symposia, provide them with research reports, and give them subscriptions to several MIT publications. Through the industrial liaison officer, we also provide them with assistance in establishing further contacts and relationships within MIT.

What types of organizations are members of the ILP? First of all, its membership has been international in scope since the 1970s. Currently, it includes 235 corporations, approximately half of which are international. International membership is divided roughly equally between European and Asian companies, with the Asian membership, a little under one quarter, being dominated by Japan. Participation by members from other Asian countries is relatively rare. In contrast, the European members are a bit more representative of the European community. One of the important things to understand is that for many companies, particularly those as far away as Asia, the ILP is the primary contact with the Institute. If you go to an American corporation and a few of the European corporations, on the other hand, they will give you a list of several ways in which they interact with us—they may sponsor research, use our faculty as consultants, or hire our graduates. Considerably more informal networking tends to occur with our domestic members than with the international ones.

Another issue that comes up from time to time, which we are studying in detail, is the extent of faculty contact with corporations around the world. In 1989-90, we surveyed a subset of our faculty in the Science, Engineering, and Management schools to get an idea of the number and types of contacts they had with members of the business community. U.S. companies accounted for 56% of this activity, 20% was with Western European companies, 18% was with Japan, about 3% with some of the newly independent countries, and around 2% with a few of the lesser developed countries and the former Soviet

Union. One of the most important of these activities was consulting, with the number of interactions dominated strongly by U.S. firms, and some significant involvement with European firms. We estimate that about 10% of the consulting contacts were with Japanese corporations.

About one-third of the respondents to this survey indicated something else that I think is very interesting and important. They indicated that, within the last year or two, there were occasions when they had passed on to U.S. industries the results of research projects undertaken with sponsorship by foreign corporations or information that they had learned through their interactions overseas. I'm not talking about something that these faculty members did clandestinely or that they were not supposed to do, but rather normal professional interchange. Beneath all of this is networking that I would like to believe is a positive activity, not only internationally, but within the United States.

Since industrial competitiveness has become so dominant an issue in recent congressional debate, many universities have been criticized by congressional committees or members for their interactions with foreign corporations, especially with Japan. This goes back, in large measure, to the activities of the late Congressman Ted Weiss, who had the Government Accounting Office prepare a report, published in mid-1992, about the general interaction between universities and corporations. That report treated MIT rather well. In some sense, we were held up positively in terms of the level of care that we have, particularly on conflict of interest matters.

Nonetheless, I would like to point out a few congressional reactions that we all should be concerned about with respect to the interactions between U.S. universities and foreign countries. The first is proposed legislation stating that information derived through research and development activities, conducted in whole or in part with funds from the NIH or the NSF, may not be made available to a foreign corporation unless such information is published in appropriate public journals and has been made available to other entities, including domestic corporations. This rather sweeping measure has been put aside, but I anticipate that it will resurface. Another piece of potential legislation states that no college or university receiving federal research support could hire a foreign research assistant to work on federally sponsored research unless it could document that no equivalently talented U.S. citizen was available for the position. The concern underlying this bill is the fact that around 50% of this country's science and engineering graduate students are not U.S. citizens. I think most people would agree that this number is entirely too high. In any event, it is certainly something that can be questioned legitimately and discussed openly, which I hope can be done before legislation with very difficult side effects is enacted.

Finally, yet another model of international institutional interaction can be found in the *MIT-Japan Program*. This program was established several years ago to address the reasons why the Japanese, in particular, are able to come to our universities and return to their country making good use of what they have learned, while Americans, for the most part, tend to learn very little about Japanese institutions, practices, and technology. This has partly to do with Japanese policy, but it also has to do with the fact that U.S. students can not speak Japanese—at least not nearly at the same proficiency level that Japanese students have learned English.

In the MIT-Japan Program, MIT students join as freshmen or sophomores and spend the next several years taking a series of courses and special seminars to learn about Japanese language, culture, and business practices. However, this is not a "study abroad" program; these courses are offered right on the MIT campus. By the time they graduate from MIT, these students have become relatively fluent in Japanese. They are then sent to Japan for a one- or two-year internship with a Japanese laboratory, university, or industry. The vast majority of these students have had productive experiences in Japan and they return to this country with a much broader understanding about Japanese business practices and technology. We are currently examining the possibility of a similar kind of program with a few European countries, but that is still under study.

Finally, there is the potential role of technology in international education and research. I am not one who believes that technology is a fix for all of our educational ills, but I do believe that in the future it is likely to play a much more important role than at present, a role that can be translated to the cross-national kinds of interactions that all of us would like to see. Without going into detail, I will list just a few examples. These include the use of multi-media technology for language instruction, research on computer translation that is based on linguistic science, and interactive video and other multi-media tools, as well as coordination technology that will rapidly enhance our ability to work across distance and time with colleagues around the world. These developments will have exciting pedagogical ramifications for all of us.

Highly compressed storage of digitized information, for example, will mean that we will be able to put short courses and research seminars in computer libraries located anywhere in the world and instantaneously access them from anywhere else, whether from a university or an industrial complex. In the not-too-distant future, we will be able to use "knowbots"—software entities that will, in essence, get on the computer networks and wander around looking at what's available on various machines, knowing what we want to know, and collecting and formatting the information in ways that will greatly enhance our ability to deal with information as well as to store and transmit it.

Not all of the technology of international importance is high technology. One of things that has impressed me, particularly in the last couple of years at MIT, is the amount of useful low technology we are developing. For example, a few years ago a group of African students at MIT founded a journal that deals with appropriate, inexpensive technologies for the African continent that use local knowledge and materials. This student initiative is now a quarterly publication that receives broad distribution across Africa. I sometimes despair about the loss of idealism in many people, but I think our students are leading the way in some of areas that are perhaps as important as the higher reaches of technology.

Next Steps to Meeting the Challenge

❈ ❈ ❈ ❈ ❈ ❈ ❈ ❈

Colin Campbell

This symposium has assembled quite a remarkable group of people who have come with disparate points of view that have been complementary and have addressed the subject from virtually every dimension. The statements have been thoughtful and covered a broad spectrum. Let me try to suggest some threads that, from my perspective, have pervaded the presentation and discussion and pose at least some of the issues that seemed to suggest further attention. We can consider what attention they might be given. The objective of the day should be to leave with fresh ideas and perhaps a new zeal for addressing the challenges that we have been discussing. I am concerned that the reality of global interdependence is not being reflected in the experiences of today's undergraduate and graduate students, in the teaching and research programs and priorities of our colleges and universities, or in the higher education policies and initiatives of the federal government. That this represents a serious challenge to educators and policy makers seems to be abundantly clear.

Several well-known shortcomings of American education writ large are inextricably intertwined with the effort to help students develop a global perspective. I think these shortcomings are three in number. The first is the inferior or inadequate preparation for university-level work, particularly in math, science, and foreign language teaching, but also in other fields such as writing and history. The second is the insufficient funding for student financial aid, making allocation of funds for international activities, including student flows, increasingly difficult. The third shortcoming is the continued fragmentation of knowledge and emphasis on specialization that discourages internationalization, which, by its very nature, is integrated in concept. Most of the individuals taking part in this symposium have devoted a great deal of time and energy for many years, indeed for their entire lives, to these matters. This conference and the discussions it has generated are sharp reminders of how pervasive these shortcomings are and how they affect virtually everything we seek to do in the name of educational reform. It is worthwhile to conclude by recalling how central they are to our concern about internationalization of the campus.

I worry that there may be a tendency, born perhaps of frustration, to conclude that an effective address to these concerns is totally beyond our control, and as that colleges and universities we shrug our shoulders and say, "that's the way it is." Actually, COFHE was formed more than 20 years ago to fight for student financial assistance issues. And it has made a difference. I think that's important to keep in mind.

Those of us who have devoted the bulk of our lives to the Academy do not have the luxury of saying that fundamental barriers put the realization of our institutions' potential beyond our control. We have to realize that K through 12 education is a big problem for us. We educate the teachers and we have bully pulpits. There is a lot we can do and say about financial aid policy on each of our campuses and in learned societies. We have to press the specialization versus integration issue and the closely linked concern about the quality of teaching of both graduate and undergraduate students. The fact that these issues are undermining efforts at true internationalization on our campuses is yet another strong argument for continued activism in the cause for educational reform.

I think it is clear that these systemic problems are exacerbated by the unevenness in our institutional approaches to preparing students for foreign study and for maximizing their overseas experience, for maximizing the effect on their hosts, and for maximizing the benefits to their peers in the United States. By peers, I mean either those who are concerned about these issues from the multicultural approach domestically or who are concerned about issues from an international studies bent. In either case, there is a great deal to be gained from broad campus interaction involving those who have studied abroad. I think the same can be said about the relatively significant number of foreign students who are coming into this country: curricula content, language training, and social and living arrangements here and abroad are simply not conducive to the breadth or the depth of interaction that should be an objective of enhanced scholarly mobility. Certainly the technological interaction is not having the kind of impact that it should. I agree with Richard Lyman that opportunities are being missed. That seems to me to be the key message of this symposium. There are severe pressures on our institutional financial aid budgets and on U.S. government policy with respect to the training of individuals from developing countries. It is leading to an even greater proportion

of affluent participants in cross-border study; affluent participants from affluent countries have been a cause of real concern. But that situation does not
preclude us from addressing more effectively the quality of the experience for
those who do have it. Beyond the issue of scholarly mobility, much time has
been devoted to the effect of communications technology on the expansion
and the dissemination of knowledge. With national borders no longer barriers to rapid information flow, creating a global marketplace of intellectual
capital should be an exciting time for our universities. But, as Steven Muller
put it, access and management of that information is costly. Confidentiality,
secrecy, and proprietary issues require a new and a serious look. Inequality,
with respect to access here and abroad, can create new frictions. The problems of specialization, fragmentation, and compartmentalization are difficult
to solve.

What can institutions do and what can we urge governments to do to help
address these issues? Let me list a couple of ideas that have come to my mind.
Colleges and universities can consider, perhaps individually, but I think more
effectively as groups of institutions, developing approaches to preparation for
foreign study and to the follow-up of that study that maximizes the student's
experience and perhaps even enlarges the perspective of her or his peers. I
have in mind here the fact that when students come back to the campus they
have something new and important to add not only to their own educational
development but to that of others with whom they work, study, and live. This
something new should be utilized through various kinds of centers on the
students' campuses, through attention to current events, and through discussion of technological change. All kinds of things that I think could happen,
that could be taken advantage of, do not seem to me to be as well taken
advantage of as they should be. Institutions might also consider new approaches
for both hosting and sending students abroad. Language training has been
discussed a lot, and with cause, but enclave housing seems also to be a significant problem and that has not gotten the same attention. The whole question of the curriculum has, and I think understandably for those of us who
fought the curricula wars over many years, received shorter shrift. The emphasis
on culture and access to it is critical to the effectiveness of foreign study programs, inflow and outflow.

From my own work over the last several years at the Rockefeller Brothers
Fund, I think the environmental area is a critical and important opportunity
in this regard. The environmental questions are scientific, economic, cultural, and political, and there is a marvelous interdisciplinary aspect to them.
But they are certainly also global. And to the degree that they're global and
attracting an unusual amount of public attention and interest, it may be an
important opportunity to seize the day and to use the environmental issue,
link it with the international issue and have a far greater impact in this area

than we've been able to have before. I also wonder whether there is not more of an important counseling component to the whole issue of foreign study than we have considered. And, in particular, can not institutions tackle the problem of graduate student isolation by reaching out far more effectively than they have in the past?

I fully realize that many institutions are doing a lot of the things that are important to make these programs work effectively, but I also feel that the existing models for making these programs work are not getting disseminated as well as they might be. Therefore, they aren't being replicated as they ought to be. There's a lot that can be done. What about the role of a national foundation or agency? The various approaches suggested by the symposium participants to enhancing preparation and follow through, to enhancing experience, to developing the curriculum, would all be furthered by some kind of an institution at the national level that functioned, perhaps, in the nature of the endowments of the arts. Such an institution would have the potential to bring those issues to the fore and into a format and discussion that would move them in a new direction.

And finally, it seems to me, that government policy making requires a great deal of our attention. We should be addressing a number of issues relating to internationalization with the federal government. This is an important time for colleges and universities to be rethinking these questions. This symposium has revealed certain things that ought to be said. One has to do fundamentally with more adequate support for American undergraduate and graduate students. The effort should be made to free up at least some institutional funding for foreign students, although that does not seem likely at the federal level in the near term. The second is a sensible tax policy for students, both graduate and foreign students. The third is a reconsideration of the huge cut in training funds for students from developing countries. These are now being implemented; they are severe and will make a big difference as to who is on our campuses in the future, particularly at the graduate level. At Winrock International, we are currently sponsoring, with virtually 100% private funds, a program for African women in agriculture that has brought some of the most extraordinary people to this country in the last year. They are in the university community now and doing very important things: a lot for themselves, a lot for their countries, and a lot for the students with whom they're working. That kind of program is not going to receive, at least under current plans, the kind of federal support that it received in the past. That is a critical element, over the longer term, in the future of internationalization on our campuses. I also think there is a place for the government to encourage and support an ongoing dialogue between educators from this country and from abroad, who are concerned with issues of internationalization. We can't resolve the issues of ERASMUS or the extension of those kinds of issues without that kind of ongoing structure, and it does not currently exist. I also think that we need encouragement and support from the government for an ongoing dialog with American institutional leaders on the issue of intellectual protectionism. Since that issue is fraught with political, economic, and educational implications, we need help to bring people together to discuss it. And, finally, we need encouragement and support to find innovative ways to respond to concerns about the brain drain, which is a particular concern to developing countries, to East Central Europe, and to the new nations from the former Soviet Union.

International Opportunities and Challenges for American Higher Education in Africa, Asia, and Latin America

* * * * * * * *

Fred M. Hayward

EXECUTIVE SUMMARY

The original symposium had a deliberately narrow focus and thus the papers and discussions did not attempt to cover the issues and opportunities related to international higher education initiatives around the world. In preparing this volume, the editors decided to ask Fred Hayward, a distinguished educator with many years of experience working

Note: I am indebted to Madeleine F. Green, William S. Saint, James C. Scott, Chabani Manganyi, and an anonymous reader for their suggestions and comments. Parts of the African section of this paper were presented at the African-American Institute's conference on "African Capacity Building" in May 1993, and at a symposium on "Strengthening the Quality of Higher Education Institutions to Pursue Development," organized in October 1992 by the Association Liaison Office to the Agency for International Development Center for University Cooperation.

117

with international education in the developing countries, to add an essay that speaks to these areas.

Dr. Hayward is currently a staff member of the American Council on Education (ACE). ACE recently has made international education issues a major priority and has added a number of programs and activities that promote international education on U.S. campuses and cooperative efforts with institutions in other countries. ACE's 1993 annual meeting brought together educators from around the world. ACE also publishes a newsletter three times a year devoted to these topics. It is our hope that continued leadership from ACE will inspire and assist many more American institutions of higher education to include international dimensions in all of their future planning.

INTRODUCTION

The end of the Cold War ushered in new and challenging opportunities for American colleges and universities in many parts of the world. The cessation of superpower conflict eliminated a major area of international concern. There is a growing desire in much of the developing world for dialogue and cooperation with the United States as well as increased curiosity about our successes. There is also renewed interest in the American system of higher education, a desire to explore the basis of our educational achievements and to examine our approaches to knowledge, research, innovation, and technology, as well as to understand our problems and shortcomings. Doors once shut to American colleges and universities have opened, providing major opportunities for study, collaboration, research, and development.

The remarkable openness to the United States found today throughout much of Africa, Asia, and Latin America includes an eagerness to hear what Americans have to suggest. Even black South African educators, who have good reason to be wary, have sought assistance from American colleges and universities.

It is easy to forget the profoundly negative impact of the Cold War on access for American scholars and students in much of the developing world. The Third World, in particular, often became the battleground for overt and covert Cold War activity; American faculty and students were frequently perceived as extensions of that struggle—an unwanted interference, spies, or provocateurs. The lessening of the fear, mistrust, and intrigue of great power competition increases the possibility that Americans will be judged on the basis of these ideas, interests, values, and vision, rather than on the basis of ideological preconceptions.

Expectations that the end of the Cold War would allow the United States to focus attention on national issues, to apply the "peace dividend" to pressing economic problems, were quickly shattered by a multiplicity of international crises: increased fighting in Somalia, the crisis in the Persian Gulf, serious economic and political difficulties in Russia, and the seemingly intractable conflict in Bosnia and Herzegovina, where "ethnic cleansing" could neither be ignored nor resolved. In spite of expectations, American eyes have remained focused on international politics. The tumultuous events of the post-Cold War era have taught us that the "last" major power can not easily withdraw from international politics.

At this moment in history, we have a rare opportunity to rethink our goals and priorities in a context unfettered by fears of war or communism. In most of the international spheres in which the U.S. is involved, the major concerns are economic. The United States seeks to create and foster international trade, finance, cooperation, and peace—a precondition to economic development, trade, and investment—through openness, democracy, stability, equality, and fair play.

Ironically, the opportunities fostered by the end of the Cold War come at a time when American higher education is in the midst of a serious financial crisis and coincide with a new American isolationism; much of the U.S. population and some U.S. leaders seem increasingly hostile to international activity. In this context, it is not clear how many institutions of higher education will be able to take advantage of the new openness in the developing world or whether funds will be available to assist these efforts.

The challenge for the future is substantial—to take advantage of the new post-Cold War environment, to direct our educational efforts in ways that will assist in creating a new reality that is only vaguely perceived, to fight against a new tide of isolationism, and to do it all with diminishing resources.

This new international environment, while devoid of great power confrontations, is replete with perils of its own. At the same time, it creates tantalizing opportunities for higher education. American colleges and universities have a chance to help rethink and set a new international agenda, to take a fresh look at old assumptions, and to explore previously untouched areas with educational institutions throughout the world.

In this essay, I suggest that part of the task of American higher education is to get beyond a Eurocentric view of international education, and to recognize the variety of ways in which Africa, Asia, Latin America, and the Middle East are important to our future as success stories, challenges, and opportunities. I will briefly discuss the current state of international education in the

United States, examine some aspects of higher education in three non-European areas of the world, and present some thoughts and observations about the future. I want to sketch out a sample of what is available to be learned in other parts of the world and to suggest that it be explored—that such exploration is essential. Others do certain things better than the U.S.: conducting race relations, teaching tolerance, controlling violence, and learning from the past. I want to provide a taste of the variety available to those who seek it, to make some comments and generalizations about aspects of each while recognizing the vast differences between nations and regions in terms of resources, quality of education, research accomplishments, and success with international cooperation. Finally, I make some guesses about the future of each area and present some general comments and thoughts about international higher education and its roles in the future. I want to suggest that we look outward not only because it is important to business and trade or in the "national interest," but also because understanding the rest of the world more broadly will inform and improve American higher education by opening doors to new ideas and opportunities.

HIGHER EDUCATION INTERNATIONAL CAPACITIES IN THE UNITED STATES

The long-term ability of American colleges and universities to operate effectively in the international environment will depend on whether existing language and area proficiency can be maintained and on our success in broadening the base of expertise in areas in which the United States is deficient, especially in Asia and Africa. As we think about the future of American higher education and the developing world, it is important to take a brief look at the international capacities of U.S. institutions of higher education and at current links with the developing world. What we find is highly Eurocentric language training, limited geographic knowledge of citizens, aging area teaching capacity, and little general support for international education.

In his essay, Richard Lambert notes that the most obvious link between U.S. higher education and other countries is the 407,529 foreign students studying in American colleges and universities.[1] The vast majority come from Asia (46.6% undergraduate, 65.6% graduate), followed by Latin America (16.8% undergraduate, 6.9% graduate), Europe (12.7%, 10.8%), the Middle East (10.0%, 6.5%), Africa (7.0%, 5.3%), and North America (5.8%, 4.1%).[2] More than 70,727 American students[3] are involved in study abroad programs overseas—less than 20% of the number of students we receive from abroad—with more than one quarter (27%) going to a single country, the United Kingdom, followed by France (12.8%), Spain (10.4%), and Italy (8.4%). The Eurocentric focus of American international education is demonstrated by the fact that 77% of our students go to Europe. Of non-European countries, Mexico receives the largest number of students (5.0%), followed by Israel (2.6%), and Japan (2.1%).[4]

The great popularity of the United Kingdom as a destination for U.S. students is no doubt partly a reflection of the limited foreign language proficiency of most American students. A quick look at language instruction in the United States, as reported by The Modern Language Association for Fall 1990, helps explain the rank order of choices of non-English-speaking countries for study abroad and the primary focus on Europe. Of the language students identified in the MLA study, 45.1% were studying Spanish, followed by French (23%), German (11%), Italian (4.2%), Japanese (3.9%), and Russian (3.8%). The second highest Asian language after Japanese was Chinese (1.6%). Of Middle Eastern languages, Arabic was studied by only .3% of the total and Hebrew (including Biblical Hebrew) by 1.1%.[5] No African language had even 1% of the total language students; the highest African-language enrollments were in Swahili with 1,209 students (.1%), followed by Yoruba with 134 students and Hausa with 132 students (.011%).[6]

The choice of country for study abroad programs requiring a foreign language parallels language training; the largest number of students choose Spanish-speaking countries (the highest language enrollments), the second largest number choose France (second highest language enrollments), followed by several other European countries in rough reflection of this rank order.[7] Africa and Asia accounted for only 1.3% and 5.0%, respectively, of study abroad students, reflecting the comparably low total numbers of students taking those languages.[8]

An encouraging note is that the total number of college and university students taking languages increased by 18% from 1986 to 1990. The total number of students enrolled in the less commonly taught languages increased 17.4%,[9] although they represent only about 1% of total student numbers.[10] At the primary and secondary levels, there has also been a marked improvement in total language enrollment; modern language enrollments in high school are at their highest point since 1915—36.9% of the total student population.[11] Although most language instruction focuses on the major European languages, there are small high school enrollments in Japanese (.59%) and a start in Chinese, Arabic, and Swahili.[12]

If knowledge about the outside world is an indication of the future of international education in the United States, the future is cloudy. In the National Geographic Society's geography survey, carried out by the Gallup Organization in 1988, U.S. respondents ranked sixth of nine on world map identifications behind Sweden, West Germany, Japan, France, and Canada. Only the U.K., of the industrialized nations, had lower scores. Especially disconcerting, as Lyman has noted elsewhere, was the fact that the United States was the only nation in which young respondents (18-24 years) *did worse* than older people (those age 55 years and over) on map identification.[13] That does not bode well for the future.

Several current trends suggest that American colleges and universities may have difficulty improving their offerings in language and area studies. Existing American language and area expertise, much of it a product of the well-funded 1960s, is aging. The first area studies programs created on a broad scale were the Soviet programs, which are already experiencing the first wave of faculty retirements. Many are finding it difficult to obtain replacements, especially with adequate language training. Similar large-scale retirements will soon follow in the area programs set up in the 1950s and 1960s (Latin America, Asia, and Africa). In some of these areas, it will also be difficult to find replacements, especially for the less commonly taught languages. These shortages are largely a consequence of budget cuts begun in the 1970s, which reduced opportunities for graduate fellowships and research support abroad, and created perceptions among graduate students that employment prospects and research opportunities would be difficult if not impossible to obtain after graduation.

Major American foundations played a vital role in the early development of American language and area studies. They supported graduate studies, student and faculty field research, and the establishment of language and area programs. However, beginning in the 1970s, most foundations withdrew from these programs. By the mid-1980s very few were still in place.

Since the 1970s, federal support of HEA Title VI has been the only consistent source of outside funding for language and area programs, with Fulbright funding the major remaining support for faculty and graduate student research abroad. During the 1970s and 1980s, Fulbright funding was focused primarily on Europe, with half of the total going to teaching and research in various parts of Europe. The remainder was divided between Latin America, Asia, the Middle East, and Africa.[14]

Even Title VI and Fulbright support decreased substantially in real terms after the 1970s. By 1991, Title VI funding, in constant dollars, was 37% below its high in 1967, and the Fulbright-Hays appropriation was 51% below its peak in the late 1960s.[15] This situation compounded the impact of diminished foundation support. Erosion of this source of support continues into the 1990s.

The decreased levels of funding pose serious problems for American higher education. As colleges and universities face the financial crises of the 1990s, frequently requiring draconian budget cuts, there is a real danger that some institutions will not replace retiring area and language faculty. The risk is especially great to the quality of African and Asian language and area programs since their per unit cost is often much higher than the other languages.[16]

Special attention should be given to these areas if we are to maintain current national capacities, and if American colleges and universities are to have access to these parts of the world. It is easy to forget that as many people speak a less commonly taught language like Hausa (in which there are currently 132 students) as speak French.

Funding cuts for graduate training and faculty research, which began in the 1970s, have created a shortage in some areas of language and area training. While some of the shortage may be made up by hiring foreign nationals fluent in these languages, far too often these individuals lack training in language instruction and the quality of instruction erodes. Shortages of language and area faculty will also hinder the efforts of colleges and universities wishing to expand international offerings. It is important that significant numbers of American nationals be trained so that developing area programs do not become ghettoized and so that we continue to have American expertise to call upon in emergencies. Recent American experience in Somalia demonstrated how difficult it is to rely almost exclusively on foreign nationals in a context of multiple conflicting loyalties.

New technologies are another possibility for overcoming shortages in the language area. While some progress has been made using a variety of distance learning techniques, major efforts could be taken not only to make up for current talent shortages, but to expand our ability to offer many more less commonly taught languages on an individual basis. Our current offerings, as indicated earlier, are distressingly few. A small investment utilizing new information technologies could pay major dividends to colleges and universities throughout the country.

HIGHER EDUCATION IN AFRICA, LATIN AMERICA, AND ASIA: AN OVERVIEW

What does higher education look like in developing areas in the 1990s? What does it suggest for the future? What opportunities does it hold for American higher education? I will focus briefly on Africa, Latin America, Asia, concentrating on Africa because I know it best. The Middle East, also an area with rich possibilities, is excluded here for reasons of space and expertise. In spite of the great variation in the condition of higher education within Africa, Latin America, and Asia, it is possible to present a general overview of each area, outlining some of the problems, successes, and challenges for each.

Africa

Current Conditions. In most of contemporary Africa, higher education is in the midst of a crisis of major proportions. Anyone who has returned to some of Africa's oldest and finest institutions of higher education like Fourah Bay College (founded in 1827); Fort Hare (established in 1916); Makerere (1921); the University of Dakar (1957), now Université Cheikh Anta Diop; the University of Ghana (1948), or Ibadan (1948) cannot but have been disheartened by the deterioration of much of the infrastructure, the decline and inadequacy of once fine libraries, the overcrowding, the malaise of an overworked and often badly paid faculty, and the seeming inability to provide the quality education that was once the hallmark of each of these institutions.

The deterioration of African higher education also affects efforts to collaborate with U.S. higher education. It hinders the development and service capacities of these institutions at home, and has led to a massive brain drain. It makes study outside Africa imperative in many fields for Africans, placing a heavy burden on their country or the individual student—frequently a burden borne by American colleges and universities in their desire to be responsive to African needs.

The crisis for higher education that began in the 1980s continued its downward spiral (with few exceptions) in the 1990s. Although enrollments increased from 21,000 in the 1960s to 542,000 in the 1990s[17] (865,700 if we include the 323,000 in South Africa's 21 universities), colleges and universities have not been able to keep up with student demand.

From 1980 to 1983 alone, according to World Bank figures, spending on education in Africa dropped from $10 billion to $8.9 billion.[18] Current totals are surely even lower, since both national expenditures on education and the total portion of the budget committed to education have declined in almost every African country. A recent Association of African Universities (AAU) study of nine selected universities found major stagnation or decline in government recurrent funding in all but one of the cases (the exception was Mozambique which increased).[19]

The deterioration in the overall situation of African universities is especially devastating in the light of expected population growth in Africa from 337 million in 1980 to 640 million by the year 2000. Africa has the highest percentage of young people under 15 years of age: 45.2% compared to 22.8% for industrialized countries.[20]

At one level, the crisis in African higher education is largely economic, a reflection of the global recession and decreased demand and lower prices for African agricultural and raw materials. That decline is exacerbated by growing external debt, political instability in many countries, continued population growth, and is complicated in much of the continent by famine, war, and disease. The decline in the quality of higher education also reflects the consequences of new demands for a broad range of government services in the face of economic decline. National needs in areas like health care, food, housing, clean water, and sanitation grew as resources contracted.

At another level, the decline reflects a reduction in international funding for higher education by USAID and some other donors. USAID, for example, moved away from higher education support to focus on basic education. The shift for USAID is illustrated by a decreasing number of higher education projects in Africa, dropping (according to one count) from 23 in the 1970s to 13 in the 1980s, to two in 1990-91, and one in 1993-94. USAID policy toward higher education remains largely unchanged with the exception of South Africa, where several higher education projects are currently underway.

With the growth of universities in Africa came conflict with government. Centers of intellectual inquiry often meant questions directed to government, calls for greater participation, for democracy, for freedom of speech and press. Faculty and students frequently became the major critics of repression and corruption, and the champions of an open society. One would have expected nothing less.

The response in far too many cases was increasing government control over almost every aspect of higher education. What had been largely autonomous institutions came under political control. Vice-chancellors and rectors frequently became more political than academic, sometimes more dependent on government than on faculty and students for power and authority.

As the situation deteriorated on many campuses, the morale of the campus community fell. The human and political costs of fighting one losing battle after another for funds, autonomy, and freedom were substantial. For many faculty, survival was impossible on university salaries and a second job or migration to another country was the solution. It is estimated that 30% of skilled professionals from Sub-Saharan Africa are currently living outside Africa. This loss of human resources costs Africa dearly.

The Future. A major effort is currently being made by a number of African universities, interested citizens, and governments to re-examine higher education. Some of these reviews are producing new visions for the future and new thinking about capacity building and human resource development. This re-examination represents an important step in the process of revitalizing African higher education, and may create opportunities for American higher education.

In South Africa, Mozambique, and Namibia, extraordinary efforts are underway to question, to plan, and to rebuild university systems born of conquest into new reflections of national needs. These initiatives are mostly internally generated, although some are partially funded by foundations, the World Bank, and foreign governments. Almost everything is being called into question. Can it be done better, more cheaply, more efficiently? Is it necessary in this form? How does one get education to the people in a context of scarcity? How does one maintain quality without succumbing to elite privilege? Are there other ways to think about university education? Does it make sense to establish a differentiated system like that in the U.S. to meet the high demand for places and wide variety of other needs?

Speaking of the effort to rebuild education in South Africa at the 1992 Education Conference, Professor Jakes Gerwel, Vice Chancellor of the University of the Western Cape, framed the debate by asking:

> How can we intervene to begin the construction of an education system which will contribute to the tasks of national development in a democratic society and, at the same time, address the deep rooted problems of race, gender and class inequalities generated by apartheid?[21]

In South Africa, the National Education Coordinating Committee (NECC) has organized a series of impressive studies on all levels of education. The *National Education Policy Investigation: Post Secondary Education Report* came out in December 1992.[22] It is an ambitious effort to rethink the whole system of higher education in South Africa as the nation makes the transition to majority rule.

The Association of African Universities (AAU), which is the only continent-wide organization of higher education in Africa, has launched a major project to help revitalize higher education. The AAU has begun a series of studies and reviews designed to help chart a new course for higher education.

National education commissions are at work in several African countries, including Nigeria and Kenya. In both cases major reviews of higher education have taken place. There are other major reviews of higher education underway. In Tanzania, a task force is focusing on the needs of education for the twenty-first century; in Senegal, in April 1992, a national consultation on higher education was begun; in Zambia, a working group has been set up to review higher education policy; Botswana has established a university task force to address recommendations following an external review; Edouarto Mondlane University in Mozambique has completed its strategic plan; and Ghana has embarked on a massive tertiary education program (with World Bank assistance), which includes the establishment of a new university.[23]

Perhaps most impressive are the countless faculty members with their own capacity building efforts, who are working under adverse conditions in all parts of Africa, providing high quality instruction and guidance in spite of the odds. One sees biological science faculty members at Njala in Sierra Leone, teaching labs during the two hours a day the college has electricity and water, lecturing and helping students in five labs being run simultaneously. Students are 10 to a single lab space, hanging out the windows, straining to see, taking notes without lab books while asking questions and audibly sharing the excitement of discovery. There are similar scenes at the University of the North in South Africa and at countless other institutions.

These are but a sampling of the efforts underway in many parts of Africa. The prospects for the future of higher education are mixed. It is clear that there will be few new sources of funding and that improvements will have to be funded by economizing and diversifying sources of income, including increased student fees, greater assistance from alumni, and greater funding support from the community. In the context of the current economic crisis in Africa, there will not be enough funding forthcoming in most countries. The alternative sources, primarily foreign governments, foundations, and other donor support, do not seem to be hopeful options at the moment for Africa because of international economic difficulties and the higher priority given other areas of the world. The World Bank seems to be returning to its earlier stance of downplaying assistance to higher education in favor of basic education.

There are also areas of great promise, South Africa among them. If the transition efforts succeed in building a high quality system of higher education open to everyone, the system will serve as a model for much of the rest of Africa. The prospects are also excellent in Botswana, Ghana, and Mozambique. The rebuilding and revitalization of higher education in other areas, like Kenya, Nigeria, Sierra Leone, and Cote d'Ivoire, are dependent on success in resolving difficult political situations.

These efforts at revitalization suggest new opportunities for cooperation and collaboration for American colleges and universities in many African nations. At the same time, there continue to be substantial risks involved in ties with some others. For success, cooperation must have mutual benefits for both partners and be entered into in a framework of equality. Participating American universities must also pay special attention to preparation for linkages, including choice of institutions, political conditions, and language and cultural preparation of their students and faculty.[24] The door is open to American higher education in ways it has not been since the 1960s. Both the challenges and the potential rewards of success are substantial.

Latin America

Current Conditions. Higher education in Latin America has grown at remarkable rates in recent years to the point that enrollment ratios are among the highest in the developing world—12% of school-age children compared to a 6.9% average in the Third World. The enrollment ratio is 21% of school-age children for developed countries.[25] In Latin America, enrollments increased tenfold between 1960 and 1985, from 567,000 to 6,416,000.[26] Funding increases did not keep up with enrollments during the same period. Tight budgets are reflected in low salaries at most colleges and universities, making it difficult to attract high quality full-time faculty. In Mexico, for example, 73% of the faculty are part-time; many have no Ph.D.s, and significant numbers have only undergraduate degrees as their highest level of education.[27]

The dependence on large numbers of part-time faculty, in Latin America generally, is having a major effect on the character of higher education institutions as well as on the amount and quality of research. Graduate study is not as well developed in Latin America as it is in Europe or the United States. This lack of development has an impact on the research climate. Graduate study tends to focus around a major professor rather than on a broad program of courses.

Low expenditures on research and development in Latin America also affect the pool of funding available for university research. At .49% of GNP, Latin America is only slightly higher than Africa, which is .36% of GNP. The industrialized world spends 2.23% of GNP for research and development.[28] An unusually large part of research and development in Latin America is carried on outside colleges and universities, further limiting the opportunity of higher education to benefit and contribute. Research in Latin America is increasingly concentrated in four countries: Argentina, Brazil, Mexico, and Venezuela.[29]

In the face of economic problems, access for poorer students is becoming more difficult. A recent study found that "...low income students are often more likely than high income students to pay for their education, and government-financed higher education subsidies are heavily skewed in favor of higher income families."[30] In an atmosphere often charged with social and economic tensions, this funding inequity has become an important political issue.

Politics are intimately intertwined with Latin American higher education. According to one analyst, "The highly politicized nature of the Latin American university is an important constraint on changes in public higher education policy."[31] Political involvement by student and faculty frequently result in closures of the institutions.

Private higher education also grew during this same period in Latin America. In 1960, 15% of higher education students were in private institutions; by 1985, slightly more than one-third (34.4%) of the total enrollment of approximately 6.5 million students were in private institutions.[32] While their quality varied greatly, private colleges and universities were an important avenue of access for a large segment of the population.

The Future. The 1990s find Latin American higher education in a state of suspended animation, buffeted by a growing economic crisis, low faculty salaries, and government concerns about costs. There are also distressing assertions that overall quality has deteriorated markedly.[33] At the same time, the last two decades have witnessed remarkable progress in improving access to Latin American colleges and universities.

It seems unlikely that the financial crises of higher education in Latin America will be resolved through greater government funding. Improved efficiency, though possible, would probably come at a high cost to access and might further erode quality. The low quality of many private institutions suggests the limits of private higher education as an alternate way to resolve higher education problems in the near future.

The dilemmas facing higher education in Latin America are not unlike those in the United States. In both cases, the future is closely tied to economic conditions, and these conditions are ever more closely linked together. As trade barriers are lifted under the North American Free Trade Agreement (NAFTA), that link will become even stronger. NAFTA should also spawn greater cooperation in higher education, with the first steps undertaken during 1993-94. As a region with strong cultural and historic ties to the United States, speaking a language known to the largest number of our students, and representing 13% of U.S. trade (both exports and imports),[34] Latin America should have stronger educational links with the U.S. than exist today. American higher education should be more actively involved in assisting higher education development in Latin America and in breaking down barriers and prejudices that have hindered cooperation and linkages between U.S. and Latin American higher education. These efforts could have benefits in the United States by reversing the growing tide of Hispanics who are becoming part of an underclass in the United States and easy prey to prejudice and victimization. U.S. colleges and universities should become much more focused on our southern neighbors. While U.S. and Latin American higher education cooperation holds promise, the lack of interest and funding suggests that the future remains clouded.

Asia

Current Conditions. Higher education in Asia during the last three decades boasts a variety of major success stories. These successes include greatly improved access, relatively low cost, and, in many countries, substantial increases in quality. Enrollment growth in the region has been substantial, increasing more than sixfold in the 1970s and 1980s in East Asia. Student numbers grew from 1.3 million students in 1970 to 8.2 million in 1988. Enrollment increased at a somewhat more modest rate in southern Asia during the same period, doubling from 3.2 million in 1970 to 6.6 million in 1988.[35] What is particularly remarkable about the Asian situation is that enrollments increased substantially while cost remained among the lowest in the world.[36]

Recent growth and development of higher education in Asia has involved a mix of public and private institutions, although the exact mix (and existence) has varied widely by country, ranging from more than 55% of total enrollment in private institutions in India, Indonesia, Korea, and the Philippines to a little less than 10% in Thailand and Malaysia.[37] Several nations, such as Burma and Sri Lanka, have no private higher education at all. China has a growing unofficial private higher education sector in which a great deal of experimentation is taking place.

Perhaps the most impressive achievement in Asia has been the ability of many Asian nations to establish a number of institutions of the highest quality, while at the same time opening access to large numbers of students. In some countries, the response to public demands for education was met by diversifying the types of educational institutions. Some of the diversification was accomplished through the creative use of distance education, some by establishing community colleges, some through other higher educational institutions.

Selective admissions requirements have played an important role in assuring quality in a number of Asian nations; admission to what are regarded as the very best universities, in places such as Japan, Korea, and India, is reserved for those with the highest scores. These restrictions have led to highly competitive and elitist systems with very narrow pyramids at the top (like the University of Delhi and the University of Tokyo). People who make it to the top do very well, but the Darwinian struggle to get there takes a toll along the way. There is also concern that students who reach the pinnacle of higher education and thus have an assured future do not devote as high a level of energy to study as should be the case.

Although most Asian nations have emphasized science and engineering education, they have succeeded in keeping costs relatively low. Part of the push for quality in some parts of Asia has come from the growing demand for high performance standards in the society as a whole. In Japan and Korea in particular, strong family encouragement and support for high achievement by children is reflected in the widespread use of tours and special courses prior to examinations. Achievement expectations have created a level of competitiveness that often puts tremendous pressure on students to succeed[38] and has become a growing source of controversy in both Japan and Korea.

Growing concern by some Asian governments about the brain drain and the loss of foreign exchange used to send students abroad for study was a driving force behind the expansion of higher education. In Malaysia, for example, where only 20% of applications were accepted in Malaysian universities in the 1980s, large numbers of students went abroad. In 1980, 30,000 students studied outside Malaysia, most of them paying their own costs. These students represented a substantial drain on foreign exchange, estimated at $1 billion in 1993.[39] Singapore had similar problems.[40] One alternative was to create more postsecondary opportunities in Malaysia, which is precisely what the government did, although the effort has been embroiled in controversy because of the requirement, since the 1970s, that education be taught in Malay. This caused concern and resentment both among the non-Malay ethnic community and among those who feel that proficiency in English is essential to success in the modern age. Those who could find the funds often went abroad for schooling, others went to private institutions in Malaysia where instruction was in English (though officially these degrees were not recognized by the government).[41] That problem has been partially solved in recent years by cooperative arrangements with a number of U.S. universities that have worked out "twinning" arrangements using U.S. transfer credits for courses in Malaysia and having part of the study period (sometimes as much as half) in the United States.[42]

Asia has witnessed remarkable examples of change in the structure of higher education. In China, the higher education system was restructured to increase the number of institutions from 229 in 1957 to 1,289 in 1960. Enrollments grew from 441,000 to 962,000 in three years. Most of the new institutions were small, poorly staffed, and ill-equipped. The Chinese, unhappy with the results, reorganized the system once more and the number of institutions fell to 434 by 1965.[43] Thailand increased its enrollments while retaining a relatively low ratio of cost to GNP through heavy reliance on distance education. The contrast between China and Thailand over this period is instructive in terms of access. Both countries had less than 2% of college-age students enrolled in institutions of higher education in the 1960s. In 1989, the ratio was virtually identical for China at 1.7% of the age group. In Thailand, it had grown to 11.2% by 1980.[44] China continues to have one of the lowest enrollment rates in the world, even lower than Africa, which, according to UNESCO figures, was 2.1% of the college-age group in 1990.[45]

The focus on quality in much of Asia has been a high priority. In her interesting study of nine Asian countries, Maureen Woodhall concludes that quality and efficiency have gained a higher priority than expansion, although questions of access and the need for expansion have not been ignored. She suggests that part of the success of higher education in these countries results from financial diversification, targeted public subsidies, greater reliance on the private sector, and the ability to shift new costs from public to private sectors of the economy.[46] The expansion of higher education and the focus on quality has occurred while keeping the unit costs among the lowest in the developing world.[47]

The issue of success in achieving high quality in university education in places like Japan, Korea, and India is one on which there are dissenting voices. There is concern that these systems create uniformity, with their emphasis on national examinations and memorization, while inhibiting creativity and imagination. In India, these concerns are coupled with criticism that although some institutions are of very high quality, the rapid expansion of the system and the demand for college and university places have created large numbers of inferior institutions. As one writer put it: "Quality is the Achilles' heel of Indian higher education. . . . The quality of higher education is subject to wide variations. The few very high quality institutions of international standard coexist with a large number of substandard and nonviable colleges and many ill-equipped universities, while the majority have indifferent standards."[48]

China, Bangladesh, Pakistan, and a number of other Asian nations have very serious problems in higher education. Furthermore, the quality of higher education varies widely, even among educational leaders in Asia, such as Korea and Japan. Nonetheless, the success stories in higher education over the last two decades provide examples from which American higher education has much to learn.

The Future. While the prospects for the future of higher education in much of Asia are unusually bright, there are also many areas of concern for the future. There is broad-based concern that the quality of graduate education, even in the best institutions, is not up to the highest international standards. Some countries are recognizing the need to internationalize. Japan, for example, is trying to increase the number of foreign students in the country to 100,000 by the year 2000 and is increasing the number of courses for Japanese language teachers.[49] China is trying to reform its higher education through a combination of market reforms, decentralization, and experimentation.

Current higher education successes in many parts of Asia suggest promising possibilities for cooperation between higher education in the United States and many of these Asian countries over the next decades. Asian nations, such as Malaysia and Japan, are eager for linkages and cooperation with American colleges and universities. The potential for extensive mutual benefits is very real. For example, some American deficiencies in Asian language training could be offset through creative links with Asian colleges and universities. American institutions have comparable training to offer Asian students, especially at the graduate level. While the prospects for American study abroad programs are excellent, American colleges and universities must do better with Asian language instruction in the United States if American students are going to take full advantage of the opportunities in Asian higher education. Advanced study in other disciplines in Asian colleges and universities would also be facilitated by a sound language base. Opportunities for research, the chance to build new partnerships, and the ability to expose our faculty and students to the diverse languages and cultures of Asia seem likely to elude far too many Americans unless we are willing to improve the Asian language area offerings at American colleges and universities.

LOOKING TO THE FUTURE

Paying Attention to Africa, Asia, and Latin America

As we re-examine American higher education in the new era, we need to devote greater attention to other parts of the globe. The nations of Africa, Asia, and Latin America have also been fundamentally changed by the transformations that have taken place in Europe and the Soviet Union. The parameters of many of these changes are already apparent. What we can see suggests both opportunities and challenges for the United States and for American higher education. The challenges will include democratization, education, stability, repression, human rights, economic decline, poverty, health, mass migration (both economic and political), and the environment—all of which will put our beliefs, creativity, and resolve to the test. The opportunities will also cover a broad range of economic, political, and social issues. They will include economic openings; new relationships and partnerships; a chance to encourage freedom, justice, and democratization; and the possibility for new vision and new discoveries. There is a danger that we will miss out on important potential opportunities because of our current Eurocentric predilections and focus. If we miss the opportunities, we will be left primarily with the problems that can not be ignored, such as Somalia. These come at high cost, are played out in a context of limited understanding on all sides, and run the risk of substantial moral and political risks for those involved.

Some Thoughts about Major Issues and Opportunities

Under the changed conditions of the international system, what might the future hold for higher education? What might be the impact of the new order for the United States? for Africa, Asia, and Latin America? What scenarios might we envision about the world impact of U.S. higher education in the context of this new order? What does looking ahead suggest about how we might prepare colleges and universities to play a useful part in shaping the future?

One of the challenges for the new era will be to try to lessen the increasing gap between industrialized nations and much of the Third World—a gap that poses moral and human dilemmas of major proportions for people who believe in fair play, equality, and justice. Part of the responsibility for decreasing that gap rests with higher education—building the capacity in the developing world to allow people to take full advantage of their human talents, new technologies, and new opportunities. Part of the challenge for American higher education will be to help make that happen in a context of scarce resources and growing isolationism.

An issue that clouds future U.S. relations with the developing world is the consequences of a continuing North-North focus. For the United States and its European allies, with the addition of Russia and several Eastern European nations, Europe remains the center of attention for American foreign policy. The current concentration on Russia and Eastern Europe is having a negative effect on government and other donor funding for the Third World.[50] Concern about stability, coupled with American economic interests, will continue to swallow up huge amounts of resources for military and other purposes, hurting the ability of the developing world to have access to badly needed capital at reasonable rates. Added to that problem is the fact that the very large U.S. national debt absorbs vast amounts of investment funding that might otherwise go to the developing world and also contributes to the high rates the developing countries must pay to obtain loans. Taken together, these conditions demonstrate but one of the serious consequences of the North-North focus, which will continue to have a significant negative influence on the ability of many Third World countries to obtain needed development funds and move forward with economic growth. Without concerted action to offset these problems, this issue is likely to become another obstacle that could derail openness and cooperation.

The economic impact of Africa, most of Latin America, and Asia[51] on the United States is small. For that reason, the economic difficulties of these regions do not receive the attention of those of Russia and Eastern Europe. The cost of capital is but one of the issues. The failure of the Third World to develop will have consequences far beyond the boundaries of Africa, Asia, and Latin America. The fallout from the failures will create new challenges for the United States and for American higher education.

There is already a technological gap that makes it difficult for much of the developing world to produce and manufacture products of its own. A growing dependency on the "haves" is making the Third World increasingly reliant on the first. Development could be more actively encouraged in the developing world, but recent trends by most of the major donor nations (including the United States) have been the reverse, with more money flowing out of places like Africa than flowing in. Add the growing problems associated with the information gap (noted in this essay by Steven Muller)—troubling signs that advanced technologies are being denied through secrecy and lack of opportunities for essential educational preparation, plus the fact that the costs of start-up are frequently beyond the reach of the smaller states—and increased tensions and hostility between the developed and developing world seem inevitable.

As economic differences grow, especially amid perceptions of unfairness (restraint of trade, unfavorable terms of trade, restrictions on exports), the resentment spawned as a result may sow the seeds of violence and terrorism. Instability, terrorism, and anti-Americanism will no longer be attributable to the "Cold War," but will be just as real. As we have learned in recent years, when violence emerges it cannot be ignored, even in a context in which the political and economic importance of the perpetrators is seen as "trivial." Exploring, understanding, explaining, and working on the underlying conditions that create a sense of injustice and foster such crises can be an important task for higher education.

Without the Cold War as a basis for competition, we have the opportunity to be judged by what we do rather than as one side in an over-arching struggle. We can operate without some of the hostility, fear, and irrationality that so often marked our efforts during the Cold War. Our assistance, when we give it, is more likely to be based on factors other than competition with the Soviet Union or its successors. This should mean that the United States will be less likely to support dictatorships and repressive regimes because they promise stability. Hopefully, the new era will see a more considered, compassionate, and neutral foreign policy. It will certainly require that American colleges and universities provide much more extensive and sophisticated information and training about the rest of the world. The new era will demand greater understanding of the complexities, subtleties, and ambiguities of the dozens of national actors who will be center stage at any point in time. If we are going to understand the new order, we need to know much more than we currently know about the developing world. That will be a major challenge for American higher education in the coming decades.

The end of the Cold War has other consequences for higher education in terms of both funding and support for international education. While it was sometimes an uncomfortable marriage (as it was for African Studies), the Cold War did make support for Title VI and other international education programs easier to obtain from both the Executive Branch and Congress. U.S. higher education is having to make a new case for some of this funding, a case made even more difficult by restrictions designed to reduce the nation's deficit.

New sources of funding need to be sought among the foundations and the corporate world. Other creative solutions to funding shortages will be increasingly necessary. Some international programs can be run at relatively low cost by the imaginative uses of linkages and exchanges between U.S. colleges and universities and their foreign counterparts. The costs of training foreign students in the United States (especially for poor Third World countries) can be reduced by cooperative arrangements providing for substantial parts of a degree program, often as much as half, to be completed at a home institution. Cooperative research between American and foreign scholars can also be conducted in ways that reduce costs and improve the quality of results.

Getting out of the Cold War mind-set also creates new opportunities to learn from the developing world. And there are many potential lessons about such important issues as cultural pluralism, ethnic harmony, social obligation, and community awareness. We might also learn something about the value of tradition, age, and other philosophies.

The prospects for a freer, more open, less conflictual world are endangered from many quarters. We need to be concerned about the functional equivalents of the Cold War. For example, the real potential for economic imperatives to become equally or more controlling, dispassionate, and repressive will be a challenge for higher education. While the ability to use economic power to punish is very much constrained by the global economy, competition, and a myriad of international agreements, there are already indications that new crises, ranging from economic competition to drug enforcement, can become the functional equivalents of the Cold War.[52]

As we look to the future, it is worth thinking about the consequences of "benign neglect" in the past. Africa has known benign neglect for years and there are indications that such neglect is becoming even more pronounced today. Can part of the world truly be ignored? Can we forget Africa or other parts of the world? What might be the consequences for the U.S.?

Europe found colonialism and its aftermath both unworkable and costly, and Europe found it impossible to treat colonial legacies within its own borders with benign neglect. As Jorge Castañeda notes,[53] Islamic fundamentalism became a problem for Europe in spite of Europe's assumptions about autonomy and separation from the Middle East. African immigrants suffer from racism in Europe. Similarly, the United States ignores Latin America, Asia, Africa, and the Middle East at its peril (as it could not ignore Israel) precisely because the U.S. population is so closely linked to all of these areas by heritage. It seems likely that the impact of ancestry on higher education and national political life will continue to increase in importance over the next decade. While the immigrant population of what was Yugoslavia could not force U.S. intervention during 1993, it helped bring the issue of "ethnic cleansing" to our daily attention. The African-American population (especially the very effective Congressional Black Caucus), the Hispanic community, and segments of the Asian-American population have also had profound impacts on American politics in recent years, and these impacts will grow in the years to come as new immigrants from Latin America, Africa, Asia, and the Middle East join those already active to become an increasingly powerful force in U.S. politics.

Another vital reason to focus on these areas of the world is the fact that they are such an integral part of our own historic legacies. I and others find part of the rise of what we would call the "new racism"[54] in the United States in our failure to understand and respect the multiple heritages and cultures of our own citizens. Higher education has a responsibility to help create the conditions for understanding and respect that are an essential basis for cooperation within the context of this multi-racial society. In this era, there is no excuse for looking at Africa through Tarzan-colored glasses (or their equivalents), which minimalize, trivialize, and misrepresent the past and demean the present. We face similar problems regarding the perceptions of the cultures of most other non-European citizens. In the 1960s, we failed to realize how hard it would be to overcome our own legacies of racism and ignorance. The price we are now paying for that failure is far too high. In this respect, broadening the focus of our efforts to internationalize American higher education could have powerful positive domestic effects.

In those parts of the developing world in which higher education is of poor quality, where there are limited opportunities, or when it is seen as a key to greater economic opportunity (as noted for Malaysia), the attraction of American higher education is especially powerful. Those most likely to be able to afford American higher education are the children of the elite and the affluent. Unless we are able to provide some funding, opportunities for gifted students will be limited primarily to the upper classes. We already see this in the African case where the increasingly limited number of government scholarships frequently go to the children of the elite and where few American fellowships are available to African students in general. There is a serious risk that American higher education will increasingly be associated with the ruling elites, the wealthy, the upper classes of the developing world. Such perceptions are likely to create the potential for further misunderstanding by our own students and greater hostility toward the U.S., especially where regimes are rapacious and repressive. The skewed representation of foreign students gives American students misleading impressions about the peoples and the cultures of the developing world since they interact with an especially unrepresentative sample. American higher education needs to think about ways to insure the diversity of our international student populations.

Asia, Africa, and Latin America have a great deal to offer us as we try to become better informed about the world in a new era. To the extent that higher education can help lessen the North-South divide and enhance mutual respect and understanding, it will be making a contribution to international and domestic peace as well as to development. The playing field is not equal and that makes the task difficult. Yet we have different things to contribute to each other, and that is where mutuality is possible. Many of the issues we face—health, the environment, the economy—cannot be defined by a single country or even a region (as they could so often in the past). That is all the more reason that we must spread our net widely. If we broaden our focus we may well discover that the solutions to some of our problems are easier than we thought. Broadening our focus will require greater emphasis on the study of the languages, cultures, and politics of areas of the world we have neglected in the past.

The future holds great promise as well as the possibility of major disasters. What is new is the context in which we find ourselves—one freed for the moment from the wrenching divisions and alliances that defined almost all aspects of international life not very long ago. For higher education, this change provides a moment to pause and to reassess our roles, to look at new opportunities, and to think about the future in a different way. For higher education in the United States, it is also an opportunity to become more aware and more involved in areas of the world that have not been a major focus, to take advantage of the new openness in Africa, Asia, and Latin America.

NOTES

1. *Open Doors: 1990/1991: Report on International Education Exchanges* (New York: Institute of International Education, 1991), p. 1.
2. *ibid.*, p. 71.
3. The number would be somewhat higher if students studying independently were included.
4. *ibid.*, p. 85.
5. Data supplied by The Modern Language Association, from Phyllis Franklin, "Fall 1990 Survey of Foreign Language Registration in U.S. Colleges and Universities," p. 3. The analysis was based on a sample of slightly more than one million language students.
6. Modern Language Association, "Fall 1990 Course Registration in 113 Less Commonly Taught Foreign Languages," Table 9.
7. *Open Doors*, p. 85.
8. It should be noted that instruction in African colleges and universities is primarily in English, French, or Portuguese (the language of the former colonial powers). Nonetheless, knowledge of an indigenous African language greatly enhances the learning experience and opportunities within the country.
9. The total is 28.1% when American sign language is included in the MLA totals, although it was excluded in the previous tally.
10. MLA, "Fall 1990 Survey of Foreign Language Registration in U.S. Colleges and Universities," p. 3.
11. Jamie B. Draper, "Foreign Language Enrollments in Public Secondary Schools, Fall 1989 & Fall 1990," American Council on the Teaching of Foreign Languages, October 1991, p. 2.
12. *ibid*, tables 5B and 7.
13. National Geographic Society, *Geography: An International Gallup Survey* (Princeton, NJ: Gallup, 1988), pp. 50-55.

14. Totals derived from: Richard D. Lambert, et al., *Beyond Growth: The Next Stage in Language and Area Studies*, Association of American Universities, April 1984, Appendix F.

15. "Recommendations on the Preauthorization of the Higher Education Act of 1965, as Amended for Title VI, International Education Programs and Fulbright-Hays (102(b)(6))," Interassociation Task Force on HEA-Title VI, Fulbright-Hays (102(b)(6)), May 1991, Appendixes A and D.

16. Fred M. Hayward and Paul Beckett, "The Cost of Teaching African Languages: Major Problems and Their National Implications" *African Studies Occasional Papers*, University of Wisconsin-Madison, 1978.

17. Estimates for 1990 by William S. Saint. Also see his *Universities in Africa: Strategies for Stabilization and Revitalization*, World Bank Technical Paper Number 194 (Washington, DC: The World Bank, 1992), p. 8.

18. *A World Bank Policy Study, Education in Sub-Saharan Africa: Policies for Adjustment, Revitalization and Expansion* (Washington, DC: The World Bank, 1988).

19. Association of African Universities, *Study on Cost Effectiveness and Efficiency in African Universities, A Synthesis Report*, May 1990.

20. UNESCO, "Planning, Governance and Management of Higher Education in Africa," background paper, Seminar on Higher Education Governance and Management in Africa, University of Ghana, November 1991, p. 4.

21. Jakes Gerwel, "National Education Conference: Keynote Address," University of the Western Cape, March 1992, p. 7.

22. NEPI Research and Co-ordinating Group, *National Education Policy Investigation: Post Secondary Education Report* (Cape Town, South Africa: Oxford University Press, 1992).

23. For more detail on some of these, see the "DAE Working Group on Higher Education: Notes of Meeting," Maputo, Mozambique, Nov. 2-4, 1992.

24. For suggestions and thoughts on these issues, see "Guidelines for College and University Linkages Abroad" (Washington, DC: American Council on Education, 1993).

25. Alain Mingat and Jee-Peng Tan, "Who Profits from the Public Funding of Education: A Comparison of World Regions" *Comparative Education Review* (May 1986), p. 265.

26. Donald R. Winkler, "Higher Education in Latin America: Issue of Efficiency and Equity," World Bank Discussion Paper 77, Washington, 1990, p. 3.

27. Daniel C. Levy, "What Mexican Higher Education Needs Next: Planning for Higher Education," unpublished paper, October 1993, Department of Educational Administration and Policy Studies, SUNY-Albany, p. 4.

28. UNESCO, *Statistical Yearbook*, 1987. The figures are for 1980.

29. Winkler, "Higher Education in Latin America," p. 4.

30. *ibid.*, p. iii.

31. *ibid*, p. 2.

32. Quoted from Tan and Mingat (1989) in Winkler, *ibid.*, table 3, p. 54.

33. Winkler, *ibid.*, is among those who argues that quality has dropped. He notes, however, that some institutions have maintained both high standards and good faculty.

34. *Statistical Abstract of the United States*, 1992, pp. 800, 848.

35. UNESCO, *World Education Report 1991*, p. 94.

36. Mingat and Tan, "Who Profits from the Public Funding of Education," p. 265.

37. Maureen Woodhall, "Turning Points in the Development of Higher Education in Asia: A Comparative Study of Alternative Patterns of Provision, Financing, and Governance 1960-90," Draft paper, May 1992, Asian Region Technical Department, World Bank, Table 3 and Figure 11, pp. 54 & 74.

38. Some people argue that the pressure has become too great in places like Korea and Japan. See for example "Education: Trying Harder" *The Economist* (November 21, 1991) pp. 3-18.

39. Michael Vatikiotis, "Back to English: Government Promotes Bilingualism as a Business Asset" *Far Eastern Economic Review* 156 no. 45 (November 11, 1993), p. 18.

40. Woodhall, "Turning Point," p. 15.

41. Vatikiotis, "Back to English," p. 18.

42. Michael Vatikiotis, "Staying On: Malaysians Combine Study at Home and Abroad" *Far Eastern Economic Review*, 156 no. 23 (June 10, 1993) p. 15.

43. *ibid.*, pp. 16-22.

44. Woodhall, "Turning Point," pp. 24-25.

45. *World Education Report: 1991*, p. 94.

46. Woodhall, "Turning Point," p. 45. The nine countries are China, India, Indonesia, Japan, Korea, Malaysia, Philippines, Singapore, and Thailand.

47. Mingat and Tan, "Who Profits from the Public Funding of Education," p. 265.

48. S.C. Behar, "India" in Burton R. Clark and Guy R. Neave, eds., *The Encyclopedia of Higher Education*, vol. 1 (Pergamon Press, NY: 1992), p. 319.

49. T. Kobayashi, "Japan," in Clark and Neave eds., *ibid.*, p. 386.

50. See Susan M. Collins, "Capital Flows to Developing Countries" *Proceedings of the World Bank Annual Conference on Development Economics*, The World Bank, 1993.

51. With the exceptions of Mexico, Japan, South Korea, Thailand, Hong Kong, and other Asian enclaves.

52. For a very interesting discussion of drug enforcement in the post-Cold War context in this vein see Jorge G. Castañeda, "Latin America and the End of the Cold War" *Transition* no. 59, (1993), pp. 45-64.

53. *ibid.*

54. See Fred M. Hayward and Reginald Wilson, "Affirmative Action in the United States and Selected African States: Considerations for Access to Higher Education in South Africa," Background paper presented for the National Education Planning Investigation Workshop on Post-Secondary Education, Durban, South Africa, 1992.

Index

❖ ❖ ❖ ❖ ❖ ❖ ❖ ❖

by Linda Webster

AAU. *See* Association of African
Universities (AAU); Association of
American Universities (AAU)
*Abroad and Beyond: Patterns in American
Overseas Education* (Goodwin and
Nacht), 6–7
Academic fields of study, by international students, xvi, 26–27, 39
Academic levels, of international
students, xvi, 27–31
Academic libraries, xx, 66–67, 78, 88
Admission practices, 30
Advanced Research Projects Agency, 79
Africa. *See also* specific countries
benign neglect of, 136
future issues concerning, 133–38
higher education in, 123–27, 131,
138n8
importance of, to U.S., 119
international students from, 32,
33–34, 37, 111, 120
openness to U.S. in, 118
program for African women in
agriculture, 115
students from, at MIT, 111
U.S. students in, 99, 121
Agency for International Development
(AID), 13, 37

AID. *See* Agency for International
Development (AID)
Aiken, Michael, vii, 92–96
Altbach, Phillip, 16n26
American Council on Education, 11
Anderson, Malcolm, 34–35
Area studies
at Carleton College, 103
funding for, 16–17n34, 122–23
legitimacy of, xiv, 3, 9–10, 11–12
at University of Pennsylvania, 95
Argentina, 128
Asia. *See also* specific countries
future issues concerning, 133–38
higher education in, 129–33
ILP and, 108
importance of, to U.S., 119
international students from, 32,
33–37, 39, 120
openness to U.S. in, 118
U.S. students in, 99, 121
Associated Colleges of the Midwest, 99,
102
Associated Kyoto Programs, 102
Association of African Universities
(AAU), 124, 126
Association of American Colleges, 78

ISBN 0-89774-868-9

90000